REQUIEM

REQUIEM

VARIATIONS ON EIGHTEENTH-CENTURY THEMES

FORREST MCDONALD
&
ELLEN SHAPIRO MCDONALD

UNIVERSITY PRESS OF KANSAS

Published by the University Press of Kansas (Lawrence, Kansas
66045), which was organized by the Kansas Board of Regents and is
operated and funded by Emporia State University, Fort Hays State
University, Kansas State University, Pittsburg State University, the
University of Kansas, and Wichita State University

Library of Congress Cataloging-in-Publication Data

McDonald, Forrest.
    Requiem : variations on eighteenth-century themes / Forrest
McDonald & Ellen Shapiro McDonald.
    p. cm.
    Bibliography: p.
    Includes index.
    ISBN 0-7006-0370-0 (alk. paper)
    1. United States—Politics and government—1783-1809. 2. United
States—Constitutional history. 3. Statesmen—United States—
History—18th century. I. McDonald, Ellen Shapiro. II. Title.
E302.1.M42 1988
973.4—dc19   88-14033
                                                                  CIP

British Library Cataloguing-in-Publication data is available.

Printed in the United States of America
10 9 8 7 6 5 4 3 2 1

The paper used in this publication meets the minimum
requirements of the American National Standard for Permanence of
Paper for Printed Library Materials Z39.48-1984.

286823

CONTENTS

PREFACE

A PREFACE, MY MENTORS TAUGHT ME YEARS AGO, IS one of four places where a historian may legitimately use the first-person pronoun, the others being notes, essays, and public lectures. In the present collection that means the use of *we*, not *I*; my wife, who shares in my work to such an extent that I have repeatedly asked her in vain to co-sign it, has done so much on this project that she finally agreed. However, two exceptions to the *we* usage are necessary. The first is that the preface itself is partly in the first-person singular, the reason being that we simply found it impossible to use *we* exclusively and say what we wish to say here. The other involves the special circumstance of the opening essay, "The Intellectual World of the Founding Fathers." That was written as the Sixteenth Thomas Jefferson Lecture in the Humanities and was delivered under the aegis of the National Endowment for the Humanities in Washington, D.C., on May 6, 1987, and in Lawrence, Kansas, on May 13. The use of *we* on those occasions would not have been appropriate, and we found when revising for this book that shifting from *I* to *we* would be ungainly.

The essays were prepared for oral delivery to widely diverse audiences, and editing to make them into a book has not been easy. In writing for the ear, one must employ various devices to indicate transitions, to help the listener keep the information clear, and to hold the listener's attention by breaking the rhythm with parenthetical asides and carefully planned ad libs. Such devices are ungraceful when read rather than heard. Again, when giving a variety of different lectures on overlapping subjects, it is often necessary to repeat passages to make each a complete whole; but readers will tolerate a minimum of repetition in a single volume. And one does not bother to document lectures unless they are to be delivered on a panel with critics, whereas readers often want to inspect the sources. In regard to each of these problems and others as well, we have striven to accommodate the reader without sacrificing the integrity of the original performance. We have also sought—without pretending that this is anything other than a collection of essays on related themes—to make the whole as cohesive and integrated as possible.

What we have done may be clarified by brief comments on each of the essays after the first. The second, "A New Order for the Ages," is a narrative account of how the Constitution came to be written, told in considerable measure through quotations from contemporaries. It derives its structure from a movie script we wrote for Liberty Fund called *A Design for Liberty*. When the bicentennial season approached and I was invited to deliver a large number of commemorative addresses to general audiences, we decided to create a standard set piece by greatly expanding the script and using entirely new quotations. (We came to refer to it as "Hello, My Name Is," for the folder in which I carried it about the country bore a red-and-white tag so inscribed.) In 1987 the address was published by *The World & I*, a publication of News World Communications, whereupon Ellen introduced yet another set of quotations so that it would sound fresh even to someone who had read the article. The storehouse of relevant materials is so rich and her notes are so full that she could do at least five more versions.

"Eighteenth-century Warfare as a Cultural Ritual" was written apropos the bicentennial of Independence and was first delivered at the General Wilbur S. Brown Conference on Military History in Tuscaloosa, Alabama, in 1976. It employs game theory and anthropological concepts, and I should be happy to acknowledge the scholars in those fields—except that I do not know who they are. I started thinking in those modes a long time ago, on my own and without any guidance, and I have never read any serious theoretical work on the subject. As for military history, there is an abundance of good books that we could recommend—on the American Revolution alone, the works of Donald Higginbotham, Hugh Rankin, John Shy, John Alden, and Howard Peckham, among others—but our essay is not strictly speaking military history. More valuable for the present purpose are diaries and personal letters, such as the voluminous wartime correspondence of George Washington, Alexander Hamilton, and Nathanael Greene. The selections in *Rebels and Redcoats*, edited by George F. Scheer and Hugh F. Rankin (New York, 1957), are excellent. Alternatively, the reader might enjoy the wondrous description of the battle of Waterloo in William Makepeace Thackeray's *Vanity Fair*, chapters 26–32.

The fourth essay, that on Shays' Rebellion, is the only one in the collection for which, in the original version, we provided full documentary annotation. We did so because we expected members of the initial audience, the Constitution Study Group of the National Archives, to ask questions about the sources, and our expectation proved to be well founded. Because we have them, we include them here. (What we did not anticipate was that the Associated Press would cover the lecture as a current news story and set off a considerable controversy.)

The paper on John Dickinson and the Constitution was delivered in Newark and in Dover, Delaware, to celebrate the two-hundredth anniversary of that state's becoming the first to ratify the Constitution. It is based upon the works by the biographers and historians mentioned in the text, upon the large corpus of Dickinson's published writings, and upon Max Farrand's three-volume edition of *The Records of the Federal Convention of 1787* (New Haven, Conn., 1937) and the excellent *Supplement,* edited by James H. Hutson (New Haven, Conn., 1987). Hutson's work includes a number of newly discovered Dickinson documents concerning the convention.

The sixth essay, that on the "middle delegates" to the Constitutional Convention, developed in a curious way. When I accepted an invitation from Eugene F. Miller and William B. Allen to deliver a paper entitled "The Middle Delegates" at a symposium of historians and political scientists, they offered no hint as to what they meant by the term. Indeed, the designation had not, as far as I was aware, ever been used before. When it came time to write, it seemed logical to focus on the delegates who struck a position or positions somewhere between those of the extreme nationalists and the extreme advocates of state sovereignty. Isolating them was easy enough, but when we began tracing their actions *as a group* by working through Farrand's *Records* for the umpteenth time, we were in for something of a surprise: they turned out to be considerably more cohesive than has been generally supposed. So that the reader may share our experience, we have provided documentation in the form of dates, by means of which Farrand's *Records* can be consulted, and our path can be followed.

The next three essays can be disposed of briefly. The Alexander Hamilton Institute in Passaic, New Jersey, asked me to present a paper, and we distilled it (now and again plagiarized it) from my *Alexander Hamilton: A Biography,* published by W. W. Norton in 1979. On pages 365–449 of that book readers can find documentation for everything said in this paper—and then some. The essay on the separation of powers is a combination, with redundancies deleted, of three different papers delivered to three dissimilar audiences. The ninth, on the presidencies of Washington and Jefferson, is based upon my volumes in the American Presidency series published by the University Press of Kansas (Washington, 1974; Jefferson, 1976). The occasion for these particular reflections on the presidency was a course of lectures organized by Martin Fausold at the State University of New York, Geneseo; in a somewhat different form, the essay was published in *Commentary* (December, 1976).

The tenth essay, "Capitalism and the Constitution," has an involved history. Much of it is to be found in my biography of Hamilton and in chapters two and four of my *Novus Ordo Seclorum: The Intellectual Origins of the Constitution* (Lawrence, Kans., 1985). Both offer copious documentation. The first full-length article version was published, with notes, in *How Capitalistic Is the Constitution?*, edited by Robert A. Goldwin and William A. Schambra (Washington, D.C., 1982). An extended rendition with another focus was delivered at Florida State University in March, 1987, and is scheduled for publication in 1988 in a volume edited by James Gwartney and Richard Wagner. We shortened that version considerably to present it as part of a panel on Original Intent at the April, 1987, meeting of the Philadelphia Society—and then lengthened it a bit for inclusion here.

The final essay, on federalism, came about by a fluke. During the fall of 1986 I delivered a paper on a related subject at perhaps a dozen colleges in the Ivy League and elsewhere in the northeast. The lecture was highly topical, and we had no intention of publishing it. A year later, I was scheduled to give a luncheon keynote address in Birmingham; I thought I had my choice as to the topic and assumed that I would go with "Hello, My Name Is." Two days before the conference, however, I chanced to see an announcement in the newspaper (and it was pure chance, for we rarely read newspapers) that I was going to speak on federalism. Dusting off the lecture from the previous fall, drawing on my *Constitutional History of the United States* (New York, 1982), and throwing in a few of our pet prejudices, we frantically banged out a speech. It was well received, and afterward we began to grow rather fond of it, hence our decision to include it here.

We are indebted to Richard B. Morris and Richard R. Beeman for keen critical suggestions and for comments that led to our choice of subtitle.

Coker, Alabama   FORREST MCDONALD
February, 1988

I
THE INTELLECTUAL WORLD OF THE FOUNDING FATHERS

VARIOUS INTELLECTUALS HAVE SUGGESTED THAT THE best thing Americans could do to commemorate the two-hundredth anniversary of our Constitution would be to rewrite it to reflect the realities of the twentieth century. Various jurists have suggested that the Supreme Court is, and should be, doing just that. The assumption underlying both notions is that our pool of knowledge and understanding about human nature and political institutions is far more sophisticated than any that could have been available in the simple frontier society of eighteenth-century America.

That assumption is as presumptuous as it is uninformed. To put it bluntly, it would be impossible in America today to assemble a group of people with anything near the combined experience, learning, and wisdom that the fifty-five authors of the Constitution took with them to Philadelphia in the summer of 1787. As an appetizer, I offer a couple of corroborative tidbits. Thirty-five of the delegates had attended college. Just to enter college during the eighteenth century—which students normally did at the age of fourteen or fifteen—it was necessary, among other things, to be able to read and translate from the original Latin into English (I quote from the requirements at King's College—now Columbia—which were typical) "the first three of Tully's Select Orations and the first three books of Virgil's Aeneid" and to translate the first ten chapters of the Gospel of John from Greek into Latin, as well as to be "expert in arithmetic" and to have a "blameless moral character." I ask you, how many Americans today could even get into college, given those requirements?

Moreover, though the Framers were, as Thomas Jefferson called them, a group of demigods, it would have been easy in America in 1787 to have assembled another five, possibly ten, constitutional conventions that would have matched the actual convention in every way except for the incomparable luster of George Washington. After all, neither Jefferson nor John Adams was in the Great Convention, nor were John Hancock, Noah Webster, Richard Henry Lee, Samuel Adams, David Rittenhouse, Benjamin Rush, Fisher Ames, John Taylor, and John Jay. Indeed, the state convention that ratified the Constitution in Virginia in 1788 included among its members, not counting the five who had sat in the Philadelphia Convention, John Marshall, Patrick Henry, Edmund Pendleton, Light-Horse Harry Lee, Bushrod Washington, William Grayson, and James Monroe, along with thirty or forty less prominent but no less able men.

In fine, the formation of the republic was a product of America's Golden Age, the likes of which we shall not see again.

THE ROOTS OF AMERICA'S EIGHTEENTH-CENTURY FLOW-ering are to be found in part in the interplay between the physical environment and the cultural and institutional baggage that immigrants from the British Isles had brought with them to the New World. Nature's bounty was rich in the areas settled by the British, though scarcely richer than in those settled by the French and the Spanish. But whereas the French kept their colonies under rigid political control from Paris and the Spanish transplanted entire institutional superstructures in their colonies, the British suffered theirs to develop for more than a century and a half under what has been called salutary neglect.

As a consequence, British-Americans could pick and choose among the institutions of the mother country, adapting those that were useful and casting off the rest. Among those that were never successfully planted in America were Britain's hereditary class structure; the bishopric and, except on a local basis, mandatory religious conformity; an economic order in which upward mobility was difficult at best and impossible for most; and a Parliament whose power was theoretically unlimited. Among the English institutions and attitudes that were firmly planted in America were the traditional idea that government must be lawful; the common law, which was adopted selectively, colony by colony; the practice of settling disputes through juries; reliance upon militias of armed citizens for defense and for the preservation of order; and the belief that the ownership of land, or the possession of enough other property to ensure an independent livelihood, was a prerequisite to the full rights and duties of citizenship. These, together with the development of such indigenous creations as the town meeting and such virtually indigenous practices as the responsibility of church ministers to their congregations, as well as the ready availability of land, bred a citizenry that was at once self-reliant and interdependent. What is more, the scheme of things required widespread participation in public affairs through face-to-face mechanisms, largely outside the framework of formal government. The daily business of life thus schooled Americans for responsible citizenship and for statesmanship.

Next in importance was that Americans were literate. Precisely what the literacy rate was cannot be determined: even to talk about "rates" is misleading, for they were literate but not numerate, which is to say that they had not fallen victim to the modern delusion that quality can be measured in numbers. It is clear, however, that thanks to the public school systems in the North and the proliferation of private academies and Scottish tutors in the South, a greater percentage of citizens could read and write than was true of any other nation on earth (and, I have no doubt, a greater percentage than can do so today). Furthermore, Americans who had had any schooling at all had been exposed to eight- and ten-hour days of drilling, at the hands of stern taskmasters, in Latin and Greek. This was designed to build character, discipline the mind, and instill moral principles, in addition to teaching language skills. (Educated French military officers who served in the United States during the Revolution found that even when they knew no English and Americans knew no French, they could converse with ordinary Americans in Latin.)

Some indication of what reading meant to Americans can be seen by reference to the newspapers of the day. Nearly four times as many newspapers were published in the United States as were published in France, though France had six times as many people and was possibly the most literate nation on the European continent. American papers rarely carried local news, on the assumption that everybody knew what was happening locally; instead, they reported what was taking place in other states and nations. Into New York and Philadelphia alone, two thousand ships arrived each year, bearing information as well as goods from all parts of the Atlantic world, and that information was routinely recorded in the newspapers, so that ordinary farmers and shop-keepers and craftsmen were kept abreast of affairs from Vienna to Venezuela, from Madrid to Moscow, from London and Paris to Martinique and Jamaica.

And the readers were sophisticated as well as cosmopolitan. Let us recall that the *Federalist* essays—the classic analysis of the Constitution and one of the most profound treatises on political theory ever penned—were originally published as a series of articles in a New York newspaper and were so popular that they were reprinted in other papers throughout the country. Moreover, Alexander Hamilton, James Madison, and John Jay, in signing the essays with the pseudonym Publius, could assume that readers would know that they were identifying themselves with the ancient Roman who, following Lucius Brutus's overthrow of the last king of Rome, had established the republican foundation of the Roman government. Let me offer a somewhat more esoteric example. In 1786 Isaiah Thomas, printer of a weekly newspaper in Worcester, Massachusetts, called the *Massachusetts Spy,* was seeking ways to amuse his readers in the absence of pressing news. There had been some controversy over Alexander Pope's translation of the *Iliad*—Samuel Johnson is said to have quipped, "It is beautiful, sir, but is it Homer?"—and Thomas gave his readers the opportunity to decide for themselves by printing Pope's translation and the original Greek in parallel columns.

Complementing the habit of reading was the leisurely pace of life, which gave Americans time to reflect upon and discuss what they read. This is an important point to understand. In our modern era of instantaneous communication, we are so continuously bombarded with sights and sounds and information that to retain our sanity, we have to develop ways of filtering out or ignoring the bewildering array of attacks upon our senses. Many of you are aware of the study showing that the average congressman has something in the order of twelve minutes a day to be alone and think. It was quite otherwise in the eighteenth century. There was no need to hurry in a world in which exchanging letters between Philadelphia and London took twelve weeks, and between Boston and Savannah four to six weeks. Besides, Americans had access to only a limited number of books—the library that was available to the Framers, one of the nation's largest, the Library Company of Philadelphia, contained five thousand volumes—and thus one could read them again and again, savor them and brood over them, and absorb even the most profound and abstruse of them wholly into one's being.

The content of the reading, cushioning as it did Americans' perceptions of the monumental events of the Revolutionary epoch, also helped make the founding generation such a remarkable lot of men. Contrary to a persistent notion, Americans were all but untouched by the writers of the French Enlightenment, unless Montesquieu be so considered (they did read Montesquieu, though I suspect only selectively). Some exotic and omnivorous readers, Benjamin Rush for instance, did read Rousseau, and many had at least heard of Voltaire and Diderot. But Americans by and large did not read the philosophes, in no small measure for the reason that Americans were immune to the antireligious virus that had infected the French.

Instead, all public men could be expected to be versed in a half-dozen general categories of writings in addition, of course, to the Holy Bible. They cited the Bible more than any other source, and unsurprisingly, the most cited Book of the Bible was Deuteronomy. Of the secular categories, the first was also law, including both what was called "natural law" and the laws of England. The foremost treatises on natural law were those of the Genevan Jean Jacques Burlamaqui and his greatest pupil, Emmerich de Vattel; natural-law principles, at least in theory, governed the conduct of international relations, including the rules of war. Readers could in fact become familiar with Burlamaqui's thinking as they studied English law, for it is summarized in the first volume of Sir William Blackstone's *Commentaries on the Laws of England,* a work that, according to Madison, was "in every man's hand." Madison doubtless overstated, but there were considerably more copies of Blackstone sold in America than there were lawyers, and Blackstone was the second most frequently cited author in all the American political literature from the 1760s through the 1780s.

Another category was the ancient classics. Among the widely read Romans were Cicero, Tacitus, and Sallust; among the Greeks, Demosthenes, Aristotle, and Polybius. By far the most generally read book, however, was Plutarch's *Lives of the Noble Grecians and Romans,* in John Dryden's translation. It should be noted that few Americans appreciated Plato. To John Adams, Jefferson described Plato's *Republic* as a mass of "whimsies . . . puerilities and unintelligible jargon." Adams facetiously replied that the only two things he had learned from Plato were a cure for the hiccups and whence Ben Franklin had plagiarized some of his ideas.

From the classical authors and from Blackstone, Americans derived an understanding of history and a profound respect for its value; but from other writers they also learned a peculiar version of history that became a fundamental part of their world view and, indeed, an enduring feature of American political discourse. This was the so-called Whig interpretation of history, which they learned from, among others, John Trenchard, Thomas Gordon, and Viscount Bolingbroke: the Whig version taught that history was an endless alternation between conspiracies by a few wicked and designing men to destroy popular liberties and the discovery and frustration of those plots by champions of the people. In accordance with that perception, American Patriots "discovered" during the 1760s and 1770s that a sinister combination of money men and ministers of the Crown was plotting to enslave them; and during the 1780s and 1790s a succession of equally monstrous plots was denounced by one political group or another. Nor did it stop there: Andrew Jackson and his followers discovered the Monster Banking Monopoly; the Populists discovered Wall Street and the Gold Conspiracy;

and in the twentieth century, we have had the Trusts, the Malefactors of Great Wealth, the Military-Industrial Complex, and the Imperial Presidency.

Yet another body of literature studied by public men was that concerning "political economy," the newly devised "science" that began to emerge when men started to realize that economic activity need not be a zero-sum game and that governmental policies might profoundly influence the growth or decline of the wealth of nations. A number of writers treated the subject, but only three, all Scots, reached sizable audiences in America: Sir James Steuart, an advocate of a managed economy whose work had a powerful impact upon Hamilton, and David Hume and Adam Smith, advocates of a free-market economy who were most appreciated south of the Mason-Dixon line.

Finally, there were works that bore directly upon the task of erecting institutions to preserve free government, namely, treatises on political theory and upon the nature of man and society. Obviously the ancients, along with Bolingbroke, Montesquieu, and Blackstone, had a great deal to offer. Another potent influence was John Locke, whose *Second Treatise of Civil Government* provided the theoretical underpinnings for the Declaration of Independence and whose *Essay Concerning Human Understanding* was even more widely read. In addition, there were the Scottish Common Sense philosophers, who held that all men are equally endowed with a moral sense—that is, an inborn sense of what is right and what is wrong, of what is good and what is evil—with a disposition to do good, and with equal capacities to judge whether their rulers are good or bad. It was but a short step from that position to radical democracy, and it was no step at all to the conclusion that slavery is evil. A considerably different, though not opposite, view was that of Hume and Smith, whose theory of moral sentiments held that men are inspired to do good by peer pressure rather than by the voice of conscience.

THE INTELLECTUAL WORLD 9

Before turning to the practical applications the Framers made of all this—and they insisted that they were interested solely in "useful" knowledge, not what was merely ornamental, speculative, or abstract—I should like to offer a couple of observations about what has been said so far. Those who are familiar with the literature will be aware that the lessons it taught were far from perfectly compatible, one with another. The Framers were quite aware of this but were not concerned by it. They were politically multilingual, able to speak in the diverse idioms of Locke, the classical republicans, Hume, and many others, depending upon what seemed rhetorically appropriate to the argument at hand. When the order of the day was loyal opposition to measures of Parliament, as it was during the 1760s and 1770s, Bolingbroke was suitable; when time came to break with the mother country, Bolingbroke was inadequate but Locke filled the bill; and upon the winning of independence, Locke became obsolete—because subversive. The inference to be drawn, clearly, is that the Framers, with some exceptions, were not ideologues, slavishly addicted to one political theory or another, but men who were accustomed to use political theorists to buttress positions that they adopted for experiential and prudential reasons.

My other somewhat digressive observation concerns those of the founding generation who did not do much reading. Among the Framers themselves, the obvious example is George Washington, who was not a bookish man; nor, as far as I can tell, were such other luminaries in the Constitutional Convention as Robert Morris, Nathaniel Gorham, and Roger Sherman. Moreover, large numbers of ordinary Americans rarely read anything but the Bible and the newspapers; the German traveler Johann David Schopf recorded that he met many people in Virginia who told him that a great man named Thomas Jefferson had written an important book, but he met none who could tell him what was in it. But one did not need to read extensively to become versed in the ideas of the various authors I have mentioned, for their ideas permeated the very air Americans breathed. In addition to the learned polemics that appeared regularly in newspapers, Americans imbibed large draughts of history and philosophy from plays—Washington was an inveterate theatergoer—and from oratory. Oratorical powers were especially respected and were genuine sources of popular entertainment, particularly adapted to commemorative occasions and to judges' charges to grand juries. Americans, who were connoisseurs as well as aficionados, could listen to good orators literally for hours on end. In one oration delivered on the eleventh anniversary of the Boston Massacre, for example, Thomas Dawes, Jr., harangued a large crowd with a learned history of republics in which he quoted, among others, Marcus Aurelius, Ovid, Pope, Seneca, Newton, Blair, Juvenal, Addison, Blackstone, and the Bible. Thus it was that Jefferson could honestly say, many years later, that he had written the Declaration of Independence without reference to any book, for the language of Locke's *Second Treatise* was common currency of the realm.

LET US NOW TURN TO THE QUESTION OF HOW THE FRAMers applied what they knew and understood. Their aim was to secure liberty and justice—and for some, to attain greatness as a nation—through the instrumentality of a lawful and limited system of government. In the undertaking, they were guided by this principle: the extent to which limited government is feasible is determined by the extent to which the people, socially and individually, can govern themselves. I can put that more simply for the sake of emphasis: if citizens can behave themselves and make do for themselves, they need little government; if they cannot, they need a great deal of government. (Is it necessary to add the corollary, that the more government does for them, the less able they become to do for themselves?)

Americans were well endowed institutionally and ex-
perientially to manage the social aspects of self-govern-
ment; but the matter of each individual's government of
himself was more problematical. After a burst of naive
enthusiasm in 1776, patriots—especially those who were
actively engaged in the struggle for independence—rapidly
ran out of faith in the civic virtue of the American people.
Embezzlement, profiteering, trade with the enemy, and
local jealousies plagued the public councils from the Continental Congress to the statehouses and infested private
life from the merchants in their counting houses to farmers
in their fields.

The Framers could and did comprehend this triumph
of self-interest over the public interest in terms of the prevailing understanding of the workings of the human
psyche. That understanding was grounded in the theory
that men are governed by their passions—not passions
in the sense of violent emotions, but in the sense of drives
for self-gratification, the seeking of pleasure and the avoid-
ance of pain. Some passions, such as hunger and lust,
grief and joy, hope and fear, were direct passions; others,
such as pride and humility, love and hatred, were indirect;
but either way, though this period of history is sometimes
called the Age of Reason, it was generally believed that
reason itself is rarely if ever a motive force. Rather, reason
was regarded as a morally neutral instrument whose usual
function was to serve the passions. It was also generally
believed that every person had one ruling passion that
tended to override the rest, and it was a cliché that the
passions motivating most men in government were avarice
and ambition, the love of money and the love of power.
Accordingly, when Americans as individuals behaved
badly, they were only following the dictates of human
nature.

The theory of the passions would seem to have im-
paled the Framers upon a dilemma; but some few had
contrived to escape its horns. For some, indeed, no con-

trivance was necessary. Men are driven by a variety of passions, many of which are noble: love of country, desire for glory, hunger for Fame (which was defined as immortality earned through the remembrance of a grateful posterity). When any noble passion becomes a man's ruling passion, which was true of a considerable number of the Framers, he must necessarily live his life in virtuous service to the public.

Whatever their passions, men could meliorate their baseness through religion, which nearly every American believed was a necessary, but which almost none believed was a sufficient, condition of morality. In an ultimate sense, moral accountability was to God; and that was no trivial abstraction in a society wherein belief in a future state of eternal rewards and punishments was nearly universal and wherein reminders of one's own mortality were almost continuous, since half the population died before coming of age. Moreover, American religion was Protestant, and even those few who professed themselves to be Deists or whose religious observances seemed to be *pro forma* consciously or unconsciously shared a Protestant Christian world view. A telling example is seen in the Virginia Bill of Rights of 1776, which declared that "all men are equally entitled to the free exercise of religion, according to the dictates of their conscience," but went on to say that "it is the mutual duty of all to practice Christian forebearance, love, and charity towards each other." Similarly, the First Congress, which approved the religious-establishment clause of the First Amendment, also appointed a Protestant chaplain.

The common viewpoint was expressed by Richard Henry Lee when he said that "refiners may weave as fine a web of reason as they please, but the experience of all times shows Religion to be the guardian of morals," an attitude that Washington made explicit in his Farewell Address. Yet the Founders' religion itself, postulating as it did a Great Chain of Being in which men stand between the beasts and the angels, precluded the acceptance of any belief in the perfectibility of man; and it was that, man's sinful nature, which made religion insufficient to control men's behavior in this world.

There were, however, secular means of self-improvement, all of which, philosophically, rested on the premise that the social instinct is one of the primary passions governing mankind: the desire to have the approval, or at least to avoid the animosity, of one's peers ranks with the physical appetites as a motivating force in human affairs. It was in this other-directed spirit that the adolescent George Washington could record 110 "Rules of Civility and Decent Behaviour in Company and Conversation," rules that formed a manual of etiquette for circumstances ranging from being at the dinner table ("Being Set at meat Scratch not neither Spit Cough or blow your Nose except there's a Necessity for it") to being "In Company of those of Higher Quality than yourself" ("Speak not till you are ask'd a Question then Stand upright put off your Hat & Answer in a few words"). Nor was young Washington alone, as the enormous popularity of Lord Chesterfield's *Letters to His Son* and *Principles of Politeness* attests. Every kind of social interaction—from ballroom dancing to warfare, from forms of address to the complimentary closings of letters—became mannered, structured, and stylized. And thereby, through the studious cultivation of civilized behavior, the eighteenth century became the most civilized of all the ages. Every person learned the norms that attended his station, and anyone who violated those norms forfeited the esteem of his peers and betters.

How well such principles of etiquette led one to behave would vary, of course, with the quality of the persons whose approval one was seeking. Among the harshest criticisms leveled at Jefferson by his political enemies was that he courted "popular" favor, a charge that is mystifying until it is understood that "the populace" comprehended the vulgar herd and thus that a popular politician was a demagogue. Far better was it to disregard both popular favor and its opposite, the foolish advice that Polonius gave to Laertes, "to thine ownself be true," and instead to conduct one's self always with a view toward meriting the esteem of the wise and the just. And better yet, for public men, was it to seek the approval of posterity, of generations of discerning and virtuous people yet unborn.

One more means by which men could improve upon the baseness of their nature was through the concept of character. The term *character* was rarely used in the eighteenth century to refer to internal moral qualities. Rather, in its most general usage it referred to reputation: this man or that had a character for probity or fickleness or rashness. But it also, in polite society and among people in public life, meant a persona that one deliberately selected and always wore: one picked a role, like a part in a play, and contrived to act it unfailingly, ever to be in character. If one chose a character with which one was comfortable and if one played it long enough and consistently enough, by little and little it became a "second nature" that in practice superseded the first. One became what one pretended to be.

The results, for good or ill, depended upon the character chosen and upon how well one acted it. Benjamin Franklin played a large and often contradictory array of characters during his long career, making it difficult for contemporaries and for historians to discern the true features of the man behind the masks. Jefferson essayed a succession of characters—he went so far as to change his handwriting several times—and though he played many of them with consummate skill, he never found a public character with which he was comfortable. When he retired from the presidency, he wrote to a friend, revealingly: "The whole of my life has been at war with my natural tastes, feelings and wishes. . . . Like a bow long bent I resume with delight the character and pursuits for which nature designed me." Washington, by contrast, played a progression of characters, each grander and nobler than the last, and played each so successfully that he ultimately transformed himself into a man of almost extrahuman virtue.

Not least among the advantages of role playing was that in America's open society, though not in Europe, it made possible aspiration to greatness, and it made greatness attainable. Where else and how else could an illegitimate orphan named Alexander Hamilton—the "bastard brat of a Scots pedlar," John Adams called him—aspire to and win military glory, then high social status, then exalted office, and in time, the immortal Fame of the Lawgiver, on the order of Solon and Lycurgus: one of those who, in Sir Francis Bacon's expression of Plutarch's conception, are "called *perpetui principes* or perpetual rulers, because they govern by their ordinances after they are gone."

GIVEN EVERYTHING I HAVE SAID, ONE COULD IMAGINE that the task of establishing an acceptable and durable frame of government would have posed few difficulties for the Founders. It might in fact have posed few difficulties, except that the Patriots of 1776, in their enthusiasm for defending American rights and in their revulsion against the supposed excesses of their king, committed the nation to two doctrines which, willy-nilly, ensnared the Americans in ideological thickets that were alien to their very being and contrary to their heritage, their experience, and their understanding of the nature of man. It took some time for the Framers to devise ways—and find the opportunity—to disentangle the nation from these snares.

The first of the doctrines was the natural-rights philosophy proclaimed in the Declaration of Independence. The Declaration asserted that all men are equally endowed by God with certain unalienable rights; that governments are instituted for the protection of those rights and derive their legitimate powers from the consent of the governed; and that if government becomes destructive of the ends for which it was established, the people reserve a right to alter or abolish it. Whatever the merits of these theories as philosophic abstractions, they are scarcely the stuff of which stable, lawful governments are made. As Blackstone put it, "No human laws will . . . suppose a case, which at once must destroy all law," nor will they make legal "provision for so desperate an event, as must render all legal provisions ineffectual."

Indeed, translated into the language of the multitude, the arguments of the Declaration could and did impede the winning of independence. The Massachusetts radical Benjamin Hichborn expressed a popular view when he declared, in an oration in Boston in 1777, that civil liberty was not a " 'government of laws,' made agreeable to charters, bills of rights or compacts, but a power existing in the people at large, at any time, for any cause, or for no cause, but their own sovereign pleasure, to alter or annihilate both the mode and essence of any . . . government." Acting on that understanding, farmers in the back country from New Hampshire to Georgia disrupted and hampered government throughout the war. Afterward, public men gradually stopped talking about the doctrines of the Declaration, allowing them to be muffled by a shroud of silence. Thus it was not by coincidence that the first edition of John Locke's *Two Treatises* to be published in America appeared in 1773 and that there was no subsequent American printing for 164 years; nor was it coincidental that after the Constitution had been adopted, the next favorable reference to the Declaration to appear in an official document in America was, as far as I am aware, in the South Carolina ordinance of secession in 1860.

Less easily escaped and more pernicious was an ideological commitment to republicanism. Although the United States more or less stumbled into republicanism by default—Americans had no hereditary aristocracy and had disowned their king—the "ism" comprehended a thoroughly developed system of political theory, drawn from the ancients and reformulated during the seventeenth and eighteenth centuries. It was synonymous neither with popular government nor with popular liberty, as is attested by the fact that it was embraced, at least in the abstract, by various petty "benevolent despots" among the German principalities and by no less grand a despot than Catherine the Great of Russia.

The vital—which is to say life-giving—principle of republics was *public virtue*. The word *virtue* in this phrase did not connote what is suggested by Christian virtue, with its emphasis upon humility and charity; nor did "the public" include everybody. Both *public* and *virtue* derive from Latin roots signifying manhood: the public included only free, independent adult males. Public virtue entailed discipline, strength, courage, endurance, industry, frugal living, and above all, unremitting devotion to the weal of the public's corporate self, the community of virtuous men. It was at once individualistic and communal: individualistic in that no person could be dependent upon another and still be counted as a member of the public, communal in that every man gave himself totally to the good of the public. Ultimately it was based upon the tradition of civic humanism, upon the Aristotelian notion that man is a political being whose highest form of self-realization can take place only through virtuous participation in public life. But the tradition of civic humanism, though meaningful to a goodly number of Americans—Hamilton and Madison, for instance—was foreign to the genius of the American people as a whole, who sought no salvation in politics. When they participated in government at all, they did so from a sense of duty (most commonly to help prevent government from encroaching upon their private lives), and when they returned to private station, they returned as Jefferson did, gladly and with a profound sense of relief.

Ideological republicanism was alien to Americans in other ways as well, for in addition to demanding eternal militance, it was both egalitarian (among those who qualified as part of the public) and totalitarian. As for the first, Montesquieu, who was regarded as the weightiest modern authority on the subject, insisted that virtue could be preserved only when the public was characterized by a "mediocrity" of "abilities and fortunes." Indeed, he wrote, if equality were to break down, "the republic will be utterly undone." Thus it was "absolutely necessary there should be some regulation in respect to . . . all . . . forms of contracting. For were we once allowed to dispose of our property to whom and how we pleased, the will of each individual would disturb the order of the fundamental law." And if that does not sound totalitarian enough, listen to the words of the New England republican Nathaniel Niles: "Every one must be required to do all he can that tends to the highest good of the state. . . . Every thing, however trifling, that tends, even in the lowest degree, to disserve the interest of the state must . . . be forbidden." These notions were scarcely compatible with Americans' conviction that government existed to protect people in their lives, liberties, and property or with their conception of liberty as security against arbitrary power.

Another part of the dogma wants notice: it was held that republics could be viable only in small territories and that if larger units were involved, they were best defended and held together through loose confederations. Hence the peculiar allocation of powers under the Articles of Confederation and the first state constitutions, whereby a unicameral Congress was given large responsibilities in international and interstate affairs but was given virtually no substantive powers for carrying out those responsibilities; and on the opposite side the several states were vested with almost unlimited powers. The bumbling and ineffectual way in which Congress managed is fairly well known.

What the real governments of the several United States were doing is less well known. They were oppressing American citizens under a burden of taxation and regulation greater than any they had ever experienced, greater than any that had been coveted by the wickedest minister who had ever advised the British Crown. The level of taxes during the 1780s was ten to twenty times prewar norms, and the increase in the volume of legislation, despite ostensible constitutional checks on the legislative power, dwarfed the increase in taxes. Quite in addition to the wholesale wartime persecutions of those who remained loyal to England, legislation was enacted to regulate what people could produce and sell and what they could charge for it; to interfere systematically with private commercial transactions and suspend the obligations of private contracts; to prohibit the purchase of luxuries, prescribe what people could eat and drink, and govern what they could wear; to regulate private morality, indoctrinate the citizens with official dogmas, and suppress contrary opinions; to inflate the currency deliberately to pay for the ever-mounting costs of government. All this and more was imposed upon a people so unaccustomed to taxation that they had been willing to rebel against their king rather than submit to even nominal taxes levied by Parliament; so unaccustomed to governmental intrusion upon their private lives as to be willing to fight and die to preserve their personal liberties; and so conservative that they could perceive the encroachments of Crown and Parliament only as violations of the ancient constitution. In sum, swept up by a temporary infatuation with ideological purity, Americans lost their moorings in history. And is common in such circumstances, there arose an abundance of popular leaders to catch the winds of ideology in cynical pursuit of power and profit.

Thus it was that, though we usually think of the Constitution as having been designed to overcome the weaknesses of the Articles of Confederation by establishing new power, the vast majority of the Framers viewed the crisis of 1787 as having arisen from an excess of state government, a wanton and inept use of all governmental power, and a collapse of authority resulting from efforts to govern overmuch.

The members of the Great Convention sought to re-establish limits upon government and restore it to the rule of law. Fully twenty percent of the body of the Constitution is devoted to specifying things that government (state and/or federal) may not do. By contrast, only eleven percent of the text is concerned with positive grants of power. Of the powers granted, most were already vested in the old Confederation Congress; of the ten new powers, all had previously been exercised by the states. Consequently, the sum total of powers that could thenceforth be legitimately exercised was reduced, not enlarged. The main body of the Constitution—more than two-thirds of it— addresses the other part of the Framers' conception of their task, that of bringing government under the rule of law. The Constitution is primarily a structural and procedural document, specifying who is to exercise what powers and how. It is a body of law, designed to govern, not the people, but government itself; and it is written in language intelligible to all, that all might know whether it is being obeyed.

In devising these arrangements, the Framers were guided by principles but not by formulas. They aimed high, seeking, as Washington said, "a standard to which the wise and honest can repair"; but as Pierce Butler of South Carolina put it, they worked in the spirit of Solon, who gave the people of Athens, not the best government he could contrive in point of abstract political theory, but the best they would receive. Thus, rigid adherence to the doctrine of the separation of powers yielded to a system of checks and balances, and absolute dicta about the indivisibility of sovereignty were transmuted into a brilliant invention, federalism. The commitment to republicanism was similarly honored by instituting a form of government that redefined the term. Madison could now declare that a republic was a representative "government which derives all its powers directly or indirectly from the people" and in which no offices are hereditary; and as America flourished, *republic* would come to mean precisely what Madison said it meant.

And yet, even as the Framers were rejecting doctrine as formula, they faithfully adhered to the principle underlying Montesquieu's work—to its spirit. For Montesquieu's grand and abiding contribution to the science of politics was that no form or system of government is universally desirable or workable; instead, if government is to be viable, it must be made to conform to human nature and to the genius of the people—to their customs, morals, habits, institutions, aspirations. The Framers did just that, and thereby they used old materials to create a new order for the ages.

Let me end where I began, with those who would either new-model the Constitution through another convention or continue to stand idly by while government refashions it for us. I ask this: Are we better off, now that government at all levels is doing just what the Constitution was designed to prevent? And this: Has human nature changed so drastically, or has the genius of America? Was it folly or was it wisdom in the Framers to suppose that the people will govern themselves best if left to govern themselves? Was it folly or was it wisdom to maintain that there are limits upon what government can do and limits upon what it should attempt to do? Was it foolish or was it wise to insist that government by fiat is inherently oppressive, no matter how well intentioned its officers may be? These questions are of awesome portent, for the Framers legislated not only for themselves and their posterity but also, by example, for all mankind. As George Washington said in his Inaugural Address, "the sacred fire of liberty" is deeply and perhaps finally "staked upon the experiment entrusted to the hands of the American people." That fire was three thousand years in the kindling. Let not our generation be the one to extinguish the flame.

2

A NEW ORDER FOR THE AGES: THE MAKING OF THE UNITED STATES CONSTITUTION

AT THE MOMENT OF INDEPENDENCE, THE AMERICAN people were sorely divided against themselves; but the Patriots of 1776 were, at least in principle, nearly unanimous in their understanding of what independence entailed. The short-range necessity was to win on the battlefield what they had proclaimed in the halls of Congress. The longer-term necessity, in the language of the Declaration of Independence, was "to institute new Government, laying its Foundation on such Principles, and organizing its Powers in such Form, as to them shall seem most likely to effect their Safety and Happiness." The Patriots were also agreed that the proper ends of government were to protect people in their lives, liberty, and property and that liberty was the most precious of these, for men were willing to sacrifice the other two for its preservation.

The passion of Americans for their heritage of freedom was intense. Listen to the speech of a farmer in Pennsylvania: "MY FRIENDS AND COUNTRYMEN . . . some of you are a little surprised that I, with so many inducements as I have to remain at home, should . . . quit my family, and my farm for the . . . dangers of war. I mean you should be perfectly satisfied as to my motives. I am an American: and am determined to be free. I was born free:

and have never forfeited my birth-right; nor will I ever, . . . I will part with my life sooner than my liberty." Patriots in Farmington, Connecticut, like their counterparts from New Hampshire to Georgia, resolved: "We are the sons of freedom, and . . . til time shall be no more, that god-like virtue shall blazen our hemisphere."

When the Revolution began, a great many Americans believed that liberty or freedom required no definition. Liberty trees could be planted, liberty poles could be erected, chapters of the Sons of Liberty could be formed, and Patrick Henry could declare "Give me liberty or give me death"—all without having to give deep thought to what was involved in the concept. But an astonishing number of Americans did devote deep thought to the subject. Indeed, it is no exaggeration to say that for two decades prior to the meeting of the Constitutional Convention, American political discourse was an ongoing public forum on the meaning of liberty. In town meetings and at sittings of the grand juries; in the newspapers, pamphlets, and broadsides; from the pulpits; in the coffeehouses; and on street corners, Americans expressed their views. And there was a wide range of opinion—almost the only thing generally agreed upon was that liberty was something that everybody wanted. Everything else—what liberty was, who deserved it, how much of it was desirable, how it was obtained, how it was secured—was subject to debate.

A related matter, likewise the subject of an ongoing forum, was the origin or source of the professed "right" to liberty. Americans wanted to believe that their rights were founded, not on mere will, caprice, or assertion, but upon some broader legitimating principle. Prior to July, 1776, they could properly claim that their rights derived from the British constitution and from their colonial charters, and those claims had standing in law; but independence dissolved both of those foundations. In their stead, the Declaration of Independence postulated the doctrine

of natural rights: that all men are "endowed by their Creator with certain unalienable Rights, that among these are
Life, Liberty, and the Pursuit of Happiness."

To many Americans, most notably Thomas Jefferson,
this doctrine seemed adequate, inasmuch as it was reinforced by the companion doctrine of the right of revolution. Most Americans, however, sought a firmer and more
stable fount of rights within civil society. The Massachusetts statesman Fisher Ames scornfully declared that the
liberty provided in and by a state of nature was the liberty
to be "exposed to the danger of being knocked on the head
for an handful of acorns." "There is no other liberty than
civil liberty," he added, meaning that the only true liberty
is that provided by the political or civil society in which
one lives.

Liberty within civil society could be described in a
variety of ways, but for the majority of Americans the end
was the same. Richard Henry Lee, author of the resolution
for independence, said that liberty "is security to enjoy
the effects of our honest industry and labors, in a free and
mild government, and personal security from all illegal
restraints." Others, among them John Dickinson and
George Washington, turned to the simple but beautiful
description of liberty contained in the Holy Scriptures:
"They shall sit every man under his vine and under his
fig tree; and none shall make them afraid." As for the best
means of bringing about this desideratum, a seventeen-
year-old college student named Alexander Hamilton expressed the prevailing attitude when he wrote: "The only
distinction between freedom and slavery consists in this:
In a state of freedom, a man is governed by the laws to
which he has given his consent, either in person, or by
his representative: In a state of slavery, he is governed by
the will of another."

From this conviction—an outgrowth of colonial experience—that consent was the keystone of free government
and also from reaction against the supposed efforts of

George III and his ministers to suppress American liberties, it was a short and logical step to cast off monarchy
and to embrace republicanism. Many thought it an inevitable step; as Sam Adams wrote to Richard Henry Lee,
"I firmly believe that the Benevolent Creator designed the
republican Form of Government for Man." And as a meeting of towns in Essex County, Massachusetts, announced,
"A republican form is the only one consonant to the feelings of the generous and brave Americans."

But the turn to republicanism was a fateful decision
and, as events would prove, almost a fatal one; for despite
John Adams's assertion that "the very definition of a republic is 'an empire of laws, and not of men,' " both history
and theory taught that the actuating principle of republics,
without which they could not survive, was public virtue
and a total commitment to the public weal. Benjamin Rush
described this commitment: "Every man in a republic is
public property. His time and talents—his youth—his manhood—his old age—nay more, life, all belong to his country." It was a commonplace that in a republic "each individual gives up all private interest that is not consistent with
the general good." Joseph Lathrop thus instructed his con-
gregation that every man "may render important services to
mankind [if he] practices every virtue in private life, and
trains up a family in virtuous principles and manners. . . .
The more virtue there is among private persons, the more
there will be among rulers, and the more easy it will be
for government to put into execution laws for the suppres-
sion of vice and the encouragement of virtue." In keeping
with this spirit, the Massachusetts General Court issued
a proclamation "commanding . . . the good People of this
Colony, that they lead Sober, Religious, and peaceable
Lives" and ordering that "every Person . . . guilty of any
Immoralities whatsoever" be brought to "condign punishment." That kind of dedication to the public weal, which
bordered on the fanatical, scarcely accorded with the ideal
of "every man under his vine and under his fig tree."

Basing political arrangements upon republican principles, the Patriots followed two seemingly contradictory
but actually complementary courses. On the one hand,
they attempted to force the people to be virtuous. The
Pennsylvania Constitution of 1776 mandated that "laws
for the encouragement of virtue, and prevention of vice
and immorality, shall be made and constantly kept in
force." Every state, in constitutions and legislative enactments, specified standards of morality, banned the consumption of luxuries, and otherwise encouraged proper
republican behavior. On the opposite hand, constitution
makers acted as if the people were in fact already perfect
models of republican virtue. From this it followed that, in
the words of Richard Henry Lee, "the first maxim of a
man who loves liberty should be, never to grant to Rulers
an atom of power that is not most clearly and indispens-
ably necessary for the safety and well being of Society."
It also followed that the safest repositories of power were
those closest to the people.

Thus placing their trust in the people rather than in
institutions, the framers of the earliest constitutions established forms of government which imperiled the very independence and liberty they were seeking to preserve.
On the state level, the first constitutions failed to place
effective restraints upon the popularly elected legislatures.
On the national level, the Articles of Confederation made
the single-branched Continental Congress responsible for
conducting the war, for carrying on foreign relations, and
for handling other matters of national concern—but entrusted Congress with no power to tax and no power to
enforce its decisions. In other words, compliance with the
decisions of Congress was to be voluntary.

Some Patriots feared, from the beginning, that these
arrangements would lead to trouble. As one Patriot put
it, "Half our learning is from the epitaphs on the tomb-
stones of the ancient republics," and ancient history taught
that republics invariably declined, in a regular progres-

sion—liberty decayed into licentiousness, licentiousness gave way to anarchy, and anarchy was succeeded by tyranny. Moreover, there were warning signs in the mob actions that accompanied the overthrow of the royal governments. "The same state of the passions which fits the multitude . . . for opposition to tyranny and oppression," Hamilton warned, "very naturally leads them to a contempt and disregard for all authority"; when minds are "loosened from their attachment to ancient establishments and courses, they seem to grow giddy and are apt to run into anarchy." Theophilus Parsons suggested that Americans had "already degenerated" from the morality and patriotism of their ancestors, and he prophesied that "in a century . . . we shall be a corrupt, luxurious people."

Things in fact began to go wrong, not in a hundred years, but in less than a hundred days after independence was declared. The American army under General Washington was forced to evacuate New York and retreat to Pennsylvania. Part of the army failed to make it; the remainder was a shambles. Congress, lacking power to draft recruits and fearing that standing armies were dangerous to liberty, provided only for short-term enlistments. Congress counted heavily on militiamen, or citizen-soldiers, but according to private Joseph Plumb Martin, "the demons of fear and disorder seemed to take possession" of the militia. What made everything worse was that large numbers of civilians, upon seeing the British army, suddenly lost their taste for independence and went over to the enemy.

Washington headed off immediate disaster by a bold stroke. On Christmas night he crossed the ice-choked Delaware River and made a surprise attack on the British garrison in Trenton, New Jersey. Popular morale improved, and many volunteers joined the army. Even so, by the summer of 1777, Washington knew that he would never have enough strength to defeat the British head-on. Instead, he would have to maneuver carefully and wait, possibly for years, until the British made some blunder that would give him the opportunity for a decisive attack.

But it cost a great deal of money to keep an army in the field, and the Congress had very little. The states were supposedly required to pay quotas assessed by Congress, but the states rarely paid in full. Patriotic citizens made loans by buying bonds, but that source soon ran dry. Congress raised funds by printing money that was backed by nothing but a vague promise to redeem in gold some day, and the paper rapidly lost its value. Soon a dollar bill was worth only two cents, and then nothing at all (giving rise to the expression we still hear occasionally, "Not worth a continental").

In the fall of 1777 Horatio Gates won a major victory in upstate New York, but his jealousy of Washington kept Gates from cooperating with the main army, and as a result, the British took Philadelphia. Washington's army retreated to Valley Forge, where it endured a winter under conditions quite as dreadful as legend holds them to have been. A single brush stroke will convey the whole picture: Congress declared a day of "Continental Thanksgiving" and ordered that a Thanksgiving dinner be fed the soldiers. The meal, coming after two days of almost no food at all, consisted of "half a gill of rice and a tablespoon full of vinegar."

Washington, in writing to Caesar Rodney of Delaware, lamented that "the situation of the army" was "beyond description alarming. . . . Unless some extraordinary and immediate exertions be made, . . . the army will infallibly disband in a fortnight." Washington did manage to keep the army together for three more years, but the British steadily expanded the territory under their control. The low point in the American cause came on January 1, 1781, when twenty-four hundred veterans of the Pennsylvania line rose in mutiny. Congress finally roused itself and reorganized its administrative departments. Robert Morris, a brilliant Philadelphia merchant, was given the new job of superintendent of finance. By borrowing money from the Netherlands and by skillfully using his own limited personal resources, Morris was able to supply the army. Then, in October of 1781, Washington got the opportunity he had long awaited. He trapped the main British army at Yorktown, and suddenly the war was won.

That ended the first crisis arising from the failings of government, but a second was shortly to follow. After Yorktown, a peace treaty had to be negotiated. Meanwhile the army was camped at Newburgh, New York, being held in readiness to fight again if negotiations failed. The soldiers were restless and anxious to go home, but they had not received full pay in years and did not want to disband without some of their overdue pay and without the bonuses they had been promised. In December, 1782, the army sent three officers to present a petition to Congress demanding action. The officers also consulted with a number of civilians who had lent money or supplies to Congress, and plans were made to coordinate the efforts of military and civilian creditors to force Congress to act.

This was a dangerous combination. Virtually every revolution in the history of the world had ended in military dictatorship, and now it appeared as if the American Revolution might end that way, too. The crisis reached a climax early in 1783, when two anonymous pamphlets were circulated among the officers. One proposed that, should fighting resume, the army head for the wilderness and abandon the nation; should peace be agreed to, the address went on, "You have arms in your hands, . . . never sheath the sword, until you have obtained full and ample justice." The second pamphlet called a meeting, where plans would be made to overpower Congress by force.

To the surprise of the mutineers, Washington showed up at the meeting. He had written a short speech, and when he took it from his coat pocket, he reached in with his other hand and drew out a pair of eyeglasses, which only a few close friends knew he needed. He began, "Gentlemen, you will permit me to put on my spectacles, for I have not only grown gray, but almost blind, in the service of my country. . . . This dreadful alternative, of either deserting our Country in the extremest hour of her distress, or turning our arms against it, . . . has something so shocking in it, that humanity revolts at the idea. . . . I spurn it," as must every man "who regards that liberty, and reveres that justice for which we contend." The officers wept tears of shame, and the mutiny was dissolved. As Thomas Jefferson remarked later, "The moderation and virtue of one man probably prevented this Revolution from being closed by a subversion of the liberty it was intended to establish."

During the next few years, some states functioned reasonably well, but others fell nearly into chaos. In the Tennessee territory of North Carolina, settlers proclaimed themselves the State of Franklin; the governor of North Carolina declared them to be in a state of rebellion and sent militia to suppress them. Vermont, which was claimed by New York, New Hampshire, and Massachusetts, denied the authority of all three and set itself up as an independent republic. Connecticut claimed sizable portions of Pennsylvania, and its efforts to seize the land involved the two states, off and on, in a minor shooting war. And Rhode Island, often called "Rogue's Island," was ever "The Quintessence of Villainy."

On the national level, the Confederation Congress limped along, unable to pay its debts or solve its other problems. Jacob Read described to James Madison the functioning of the Congress: "We debate, make and hear long and often Spirited Speeches, but when the Moment arrives for a Vote *We Adjourn*." Congressman Rufus King, soon to be a member of the Constitutional Convention, wrote to his colleague Elbridge Gerry, "The treasury now is literally without a penny."

In September, 1786, a handful of men acting in the

name of the nation took a step toward finding a happier solution. A convention of delegates from five states met in Annapolis, Maryland, to discuss commercial problems. When they arrived, Madison, along with Hamilton and Dickinson, urged that a circular letter be sent to Congress and to the state governors, asking for a general convention to meet in Philadelphia the next spring to revise the American system of government.

Initially, most of the state governments reacted negatively to the call for a general convention. The Congress referred the proposal to a committee of three, which referred it to a committee of thirteen, which was never appointed.

Madison and others were becoming genuinely alarmed by the urgency of the situation and the dire possibilities. "The Present System," he wrote, cannot "last long under these circumstances. . . . A propensity toward Monarchy is said to have been produced . . . in some leading minds. The bulk of the people will probably prefer the lesser evil of a partition of the Union" into regional confederations. But he continued, "Tho' it is a lesser evil, it is so great a one that I hope the danger of it will rouse all the real friends of the Revolution to . . . redeem the honor of the Republican name." As Benjamin Rush commented, "A bramble will exercise dominion over us, if we neglect any longer to choose a vine or a fig-tree for that purpose."

Then, in the winter of 1786, troubles arose in the back country of New England. In 1786 the government of Massachusetts, having taken on and mismanaged a huge burden of public debt, levied and set out to collect an oppressive and, in fact, unpayable array of taxes to service that debt. In response, large bands of horsemen rode about that fall, closing the county courts to prevent the collection of taxes. Emboldened by their success, they began forming themselves into regular military companies under the leadership of Daniel Shays and other former officers of the Continental line, and there were rumors that they planned to march on Boston to plunder the state capital. Liberty seemed indeed to be degenerating into anarchy.

Washington, in retirement at Mount Vernon, was informed—actually misinformed—about Shays' Rebellion by Superintendent of War Henry Knox, and Washington spread the news to friends throughout the country. He repeated Knox's claim that the Shaysites "constitute a body of twelve or fifteen thousand desperate" men. "How melancholy," Washington continued, "that in so short a space, we should have made such large strides toward fulfilling the prediction of our transatlantic foe! 'Leave them to themselves, and their government will soon dissolve.' "

The news of Shays' Rebellion came at the same time as news of the final, absolute rejection of an amendment to the Articles of Confederation that would have provided Congress with a limited power of taxation. The states were jolted into action: by spring, all but Rhode Island had chosen representatives to the Grand Convention.

The convention began its work at the end of May. "The eyes of the United States are turned upon this assembly," wrote George Mason, a delegate from Virginia, "and their expectations raised to a very anxious degree. May God grant, we may be able to gratify them, by establishing a wise and just government."

The convention worked in secret, behind closed doors. Thus being freed from the constraints of "the gallery," the delegates were able to regard posterity as their true constituency. And not a word of the proceedings was leaked to the press. That was an indispensible condition of success: had the nation known of the intense disagreements, sometimes broadly philosophical and sometimes narrowly interested, that often characterized the debates, it seems likely that nothing could have been accomplished.

All that was known was the personnel, and that was reassuring. An article in the *Pennsylvania Journal* on May 30, which was reprinted in some thirty other newspapers, listed some of the delegates and maintained that "perhaps no age or country ever saw more wisdom, patriotism and probity united in a single assembly, than we now behold in the convention of the states." Though the convention followed the congressional rule that each state delegation have one vote, the delegations ranged in size from New Hampshire's two to Pennsylvania's eight. Fifty-five men participated at one time or another, the average attendance being about forty. There are thirty-nine signatures on the finished document. The delegates were extremely learned but also thoroughly practical men of the world, whose combined experience in law, trade, farming, war, and politics was astonishing. A few of them were men of mediocre talents, but most were highly able, and upwards of a dozen were truly awesome.

The work of the convention unfolded in four broad phases. In the first, which lasted just under two months, the delegates agreed to disregard their instructions, which authorized them only to propose amendments to the Articles of Confederation, and to propose an entirely new constitution instead. The most important substantive decision made during this period was to establish a bicameral legislature, one branch representing people and the other representing state governments. During the second phase, which lasted from July 26 to August 5, the convention took a recess and turned its resolutions over to a committee of detail, which fashioned a rough draft of a constitution. In the third phase, August 6 to September 10, flesh and blood were added to the constitutional skeleton: the form of the judicial and executive branches was agreed upon, and it was determined which branches of which governments should have what powers and what powers should be denied. The final phase was the work of a five-man committee of style, which wrote the finished product.

On September 17, 1787, the work was completed. The convention had produced something unprecedented in all the ages: a limited government under law, which is to say that the Constitution is a law *governing government itself.* Just how limited the national government was designed to be can be illustrated by a discussion that took place on August 7. It had been proposed that Congress should be required to meet at least once a year. Gouverneur Morris, though he was one of the most outspoken nationalists in the convention, objected to requiring a meeting every year, as there might not be enough "public business" to transact every year. Otherwise, the crucial things about the Constitution are the allocation of powers among governments and branches of government and the rules by which power shall be exercised by each of the parts: the Constitution is primarily *procedural* law, not substantive law.

The key to the system lay in the Framers' conviction that the essence of tyranny was the unrestrained expression of the will of the sovereign—that is, whoever it was that had the power to make and enforce the law. "All men having power," said Madison, "ought to be distrusted to a certain degree." The problem, however, was that in the United States the people themselves, or their representatives, were sovereign, and most of the Framers had become convinced by the experience of the years since 1776 that the greatest danger to liberty in America came from the unchecked will of the sovereign people. As Elbridge Gerry had remarked in the convention, "The evils we experience flow from an excess of democracy."

One obvious way by which they sought to check that will in the Constitution was to divide power, partly along a vertical axis with the federal/state system and partly along a horizontal axis among the various branches of the national government. But they employed a subtler means as well: they divided the people into various aspects or capacities of themselves. In *Federalist* number 51, Madison described the effect: "Whilst all authority . . . will be derived from and dependent on the society, the society itself will be broken into so many parts, interests and classes of citizens, that the rights of individuals, or of the minority, will be in little danger from interested combinations of the majority."

In other words, "the people" were not, in any part of the multilevel government, allowed to act as the whole people. Instead, for purposes of expressing their will, they were separated from themselves both in space and in time. Thus, the House of Representatives, which was conceived as the democratic branch, was to be elected directly by the people every two years—not, however, by the people as a whole, but by people as inhabitants of particular areas, states, or subdivisions of states. The Senate was to be elected by the state legislatures, which themselves represented the people in their capacities as citizens of counties or towns. Senators were further removed by a time barrier, one-third of them being chosen every two years for six-year terms. The electoral-college system, though cumbersome, was a stroke of genius: it freed the president from both the immediate will of the people and the will of the national legislature. The judiciary was even further removed by the appointment process and by tenure for life or good behavior. The result of this jerry-built arrangement was to check power with power, to balance force against force and interest against interest, and to ensure that although power ultimately stemmed from the people, they would have no way of immediately exercising it.

The division of every voter into many artificial parts of himself and the division of the government into rival parts of itself was one aspect of the genius of the American constitutional order. Another concerned the actuating principle of the governmental system. Having come to realize that the almost fanatical public virtue required by classical republicanism was simply not to be found in the American people—if indeed in any people—the Founding Fathers created a republic that, though its electoral procedures were designed to enable the best men to rise to the top, nonetheless rested on the assumption that most people, most of the time, would put their own interests first and therefore that prudent policy would induce them to serve the public interest by making it in their private interest to do so.

A third aspect stemmed from the fact that the division and definition of power, on both axes, were neither static nor precise. This very fact, that power was ill defined and free to shift from one place to another as time and circumstance should dictate, made the system viable. It could live through wars and revolutions and the most profound economic, social, and technological changes the world had ever seen and be amended twenty-six times; and yet, until very recently, its essence would remain the same.

Such was the instrument the Framers handed down. It no longer functions as it was designed to function, but Americans should cherish it nonetheless and seek a return to its principles. For as Daniel Webster said: "Miracles do not cluster. Hold on to the Constitution of the United States of America and the Republic for which it stands— what has happened once in six thousand years may never happen again. Hold on to your Constitution, for if the American Constitution shall fail there will be anarchy throughout the world."

3

EIGHTEENTH-CENTURY WARFARE AS A CULTURAL RITUAL

IT IS FASHIONABLE THESE DAYS TO DENIGRATE WAR and the military ideal as being savage, primitive, and, at the same time, somehow unnatural and inhuman. This is not only a logically inconsistent position; it also shows a lack of knowledge of history and equally a lack of understanding of the human condition. The truth is that war—as we shall see through a survey of its conduct during the eighteenth century—has in the Western world had a civilizing influence, serving as a socially useful check upon the innate violence of man's nature.

To understand that proposition, one must think of war as a game, disregarding the artificial distinction that is ordinarily made between those activities that we call games and those that we think of as reality. We regard politics, war, and courtroom trials as "real"; and we regard football, baseball, and parcheesi as games. We would normally justify the distinction on grounds something like this: if the activity is pursued for its own sake and if the rewards of success are merely psychic—in other words, if we do it for fun—then we regard the contest as a game. If, on the other hand, skillful or successful playing is rewarded with wealth, prestige, or power, we regard the activity as real. But a moment's reflection will reveal the shortcomings of that basis of distinction, for in those terms, football and baseball have nowadays become more "real" than politics and war.

Rather, games should be defined as follows. They are social rituals whose functions are to organize and channel and to release and/or sharpen the aggressive, competitive instincts that all humans possess to a greater or lesser degree and that, if not so directed, would be turned to random and socially destructive ends. Secondarily, games function as rites of passage or of purification—directly for the players and, what is socially more important, vicariously for spectators who identify with groups of contestants. In that spirit, we might count as games, without prejudice, war as well as football, politics as well as soccer, playing the stock market as well as playing tennis.

To qualify as games, ritual contests must have a number of special characteristics. They must have rules and conventions which not only govern the course of the contest itself but also assign stylized role-playing forms of behavior to the participants. Team games are normally territorial, which is to say that they are played in a designated area, beyond which no activity that affects the outcome is permissible, though conferences on strategy and tactics are not confined to the playing zone. Teams normally represent specific geopolitical entities and consist only of players who wear uniforms and use acceptable equipment. Games are begun at times agreed upon in advance, or by the performance of certain rituals, or by the observance of certain conventions; action can be halted and resumed in accordance with other rules and ceremonies. The game may or may not have time limits. If not, it ends when one side or the other wins, or it is agreed that the contest is a draw. Winning can be accomplished in various ways, depending upon the nature and rules of the game: by accumulating the greatest number of counters, by arriving first at a particular destination, by gaining control of specified areas, by disqualifying a sufficient number of opposing players, by destroying the opponent's willingness to continue playing. Most importantly, a game is organized, disciplined, and structured, no matter how much mayhem takes place during the periods of action. It is civilized, as opposed to natural, spontaneous, random, savage, or barbarian.

From the foregoing, it should be obvious that warfare may or may not be a game, depending upon the way it is conducted. Notice the use of the word *warfare*, not the word *war*. Warfare, meaning group fighting with the intent to subdue, wound, or kill members of alien groups, is very nearly universal; war is largely a social invention of the Western world and has traditionally been fought only in the West or among imitators of the West. Nor, even in the West, has warfare always been the civilized game of war. The ancient Celts, who fought in the nude as late as the fifth and sixth centuries, their bodies garishly painted blue and their ferocity mitigated by neither mercy nor concern for the lives of women and children, were certainly not playing a game with rules. Nor can *war* or *game* be used to describe the brutal warfare that characterized the early Middle Ages throughout Europe or the Mongol invasions that ravaged Europe during the thirteenth century—though in view of the way the Mongols celebrated their conquests (pillaging towns, engaging in drunken revelries, and raping every female in sight), one might infer that they enjoyed what they were doing even if, strictly speaking, it did not qualify as a game.

Whether warfare is to function as a game depends upon an interplay between technology and what a society regards as the legitimate objectives of group combat. When the technology is excessively deadly, the fighting is less likely to be a game than when the technology is not especially lethal. Warfare against the English long bow, for instance, was not a game; it was suicide. Armor, on the other hand, was a greatly civilizing innovation, for as King James I remarked, "Armor provided double protection—first it kept a knight from being injured, and second, it kept him from injuring anybody else."

The other determinant, the socially derived definition of the objectives, is more complex, but its principles can be stated simply. If the object is tangible—for example, the acquisition of territory, status, or wealth—the contest is likely to be a civilized game. If the object is emotional, religious, or ideological, the exercise of restraint, whether through rules or chivalrous behavior, is far less likely to be present, and therefore the fighting is far more likely to be barbarous.

Of the two sets of determinants, the latter is considerably more important: the determination to kill the enemy, as opposed to racking up counters in the game so as to win lands or riches from him, can go a long way toward making up for technological shortcomings. The warfare of the mid seventeenth century affords an instructive example. When the English Civil War began in 1642, the technology of warfare was actually less deadly than it had been two or three centuries earlier. To be sure, the technology of the siege had recently been improved somewhat through the introduction of mining, but that of the "set-piece" or "pitched" battle was so crude as to be almost comical. The musket had replaced the arquebus, but the light musket, the flintlock, and the bayonet had not yet been invented. The cumbersome matchlock musket, mounted on a rest and capable of being fired, with luck, at the rate of one round every two minutes, was the heart of the line; but it was so ineffective that musketeers had to be protected by pikemen armed with sixteen-foot steel-tipped spears. And yet the carnage during England's Civil War and Commonwealth period was the bloodiest in that nation's history, with the possible exception of World War

I. The reason was that the Puritan Roundheads took their warfare too seriously: they were fighting for the holy cause of their particular version of Protestantism, and thus to show mercy, take prisoners, or otherwise exercise restraint toward the enemy was to compromise with the Devil and thereby to court eternal damnation. Cromwell's legions took no such chances with their immortal souls. Despite the crudeness of their weapons, they were capable of shuffling from this mortal coil thousands upon thousands of Irish or Welsh or Scottish men, women, and children in a single outing.

In warfare as in many another field of human endeavor, the eighteenth century witnessed a happy concatenation of circumstances that permitted the evolution of highly civilized forms of activity. In warfare no less than in mathematics and music, on the battlefield as well as in the salon, the epoch was one in which Western Europe attained previously unimagined pinnacles. And the game of war was among the highest and most noble fields of all, even in an age that produced Sir Isaac Newton and Johann Sebastian Bach.

The technology of warfare was utterly ideal: advanced enough to be exciting and even dangerous, but not so deadly as to lend itself readily to killing people on a grand scale. Horse-drawn field artillery, the light flintlock musket, the socket bayonet, and other inventions added new and challenging dimensions to the tactics of set-piece field warfare without appreciably increasing the personal risks. Cannons were bigger and louder and somewhat more accurate and were wonderfully adaptable for intimidating and even terrifying the troops, but since they fired relatively small quantities of inert matter (exploding shells had been invented but were as yet crude and expensive), they were quite unlikely to hurt many people. The socket bayonet was a savagely brutal and deadly weapon, it is true, but it was neutralized to a considerable extent by the improved musketry. What a lovely weapon the flintlock smoothbore musket was! In the hands of an expert, it could be fired four or five times a minute, and it was effective—or at any rate, its balls could penetrate the skin—up to about sixty yards. On the other hand, although its soft lead balls could inflict messy and painful wounds, it was not deadly except in case of flukish shots, and it was rarely accurate at any range. It may be likened to a single-shot oversized (14- pound) BB gun that fired oversized pellets, roughly the size of marbles. More aptly, perhaps, its projectiles were like a knuckle ball, spinning little if at all and moving erratically at a relatively slow speed. One can scarcely imagine a weapon more admirably adapted to gentlemanly warfare.

The social values of the time nicely complemented the weaponry. The old nobility was being supplanted in England and Holland by the burghers and the gentry, and the nobility in France was soon to go. The newly emerging dominant classes, as is common in such circumstances, were almost fetishistically concerned with codes of proper behavior. (Aristocrats, in contrast to *nouveaux riches*, pay little heed to proprieties, assuming that whatever they do is proper because it is they who are doing it.) As is also customary, the parvenu gentry of the eighteenth century developed their codes largely on the basis of a misconception about the way the outgoing aristocratic classes behaved. Hence, gentlemen paid great attention to being chivalrous, which was a pattern of behavior that had long been defunct and indeed had rarely been practiced among the nobility, and to being polite, which was totally alien to the nobles' experience.

Proper manners were all-important. Notice the phraseology: the very word *manners* connotes behavior that is learned, imitative, stylized, artificial, pretentious, even hypocritical. The prejudices of our own standardless age to the contrary notwithstanding, those attributes are not despicable but admirable. After all, we are what we imitate and what we pretend to be. More properly, it is only through imitation and pretense that we learn to comport ourselves as something other than beasts, and therefore become something other than beasts.

The part of the eighteenth-century gentleman's code that most directly concerns us here is the preoccupation with virtue in the original Latin sense of the term, meaning manhood. The marks of virtue/manhood were many; they included a sense of duty, responsibility, courage, graciousness, gallantry, magnanimity, and above all, honor. The infusion of these qualities into warfare transformed it from the barbarous activity it had been during the seventeenth century into a game that was as structured as a minuet and as socially beneficial as the invention of the state.

To recite all the rules of the game would be tedious, but perhaps a brief description will impart its flavor. First, however, it is only proper to point out that there were some exceptions to the general observations that follow. One is that naval warfare was extremely gory—it was necessary, in preparing for an engagement, to sprinkle the decks with sand lest they become too slippery with blood—but in other respects, naval combat was even more formal and polite than land warfare. Another exception is that, in certain broad respects, fighting continued to be conducted much as it had been for centuries. The principal objectives of strategy continued to be control of cities, supplies, and avenues of transportation and communication; the main forms of engagements continued to be sieges and set-piece pitched battles. Moreover, in the eighteenth century there were no major developments in the art of siege warfare, the marquis de Vauban's great contributions and the innovations in modified field siege having come late in the seventeenth century. Perhaps it is significant that the siege, which does not readily lend itself to heroics and gallantry, declined appreciably in popularity; the two most admired military figures of the epoch, the duke of Marlborough and Frederick the Great, were outspokenly disdainful of siege warfare.

The heart of the game was the pitched battle, which, when properly staged—the men neatly ordered and dressed in splendid scarlet, green, yellow, or blue and accompanied by large bands of fifes and drums and trumpets, playing Handel marches—was a thrilling sight for the many spectators who gathered to watch it. The staging, however, was no simple affair. Quite in addition to preparations that would affect the outcome, such as ensuring that infantrymen were appropriately disciplined and equipped and that artillery and cavalry were suitably deployed, countless other preparations were necessary for reasons of propriety. Take the choice of time and place. A battle should not begin in the early morning or late afternoon with the armies facing one another east and west, for that would place one side at the unsportsmanlike disadvantage of having the sun in its eyes. A truly proper battle site also must have vantage points from which spectators—who often included the wives and children of the officers, poets, artists, aficionados, and guest observers from nonparticipating countries—could view the doings in safety and comfort. A proposed engagement would be postponed in the event of inclement weather, and the normal playing season did not extend into the winter months. One battle reportedly was postponed because a general's pet dog wandered onto the battlefield; under a truce agreement, soldiers from both armies conducted a search, and not until the dear little creature had been found and removed from danger did the battle begin.

Staging the battle was the task of the generals. Their art required a thorough grounding in the rules, a flair for showmanship, administrative skill, and wits. Wits came to play in attempting, within the framework of the niceties and proprieties and of what the opposing general would allow, to maneuver so as to obtain an edge for one's men in the form of being uphill or having better shelter or a preponderance of force and in choosing between such tactical options as encirclement, flanking attacks, entrenchment, and frontal assaults. Understandably, it sometimes took months for all the appropriate arrangements to be made. When they had been made, the general's work was temporarily done, except for being ready to send reinforcements to bolster a sagging line or otherwise make emergency repairs; and the battle could begin.

The direct confrontation of lines was the most popular form of engagement, since it provided the best circumstances for a test of virtue. As the battle opened, the troops—enlisted men under the direct command of junior officers—advanced upon one another steadily, their muskets primed and leveled at their opposite numbers, their bayonets fixed. Artillery exploded everywhere, its function often being more to demoralize than actually to kill. Now came into play the highest attributes of manhood: courage, self-discipline, and the ability to think coolly and clearly under fire. The immediate object was to "break the line" of the enemy, whose strength lay in the mutual support and confidence afforded by a well-knit formation. Once the line had been penetrated, once the enemy infantrymen found their ranks broken and saw themselves vulnerable to attack on all sides instead of just in front, their normal reaction was to panic and flee. Whether a line would hold or break depended largely upon the delicate balance between the musket and the bayonet. Defensive firing was delayed until the last moment so that the balls would be most likely to effect damage; it was normally done in unison by platoons standing two or three deep. After each volley came a crucial decision: assay the damage done by the muskets and determine whether it was better to attempt a bayonet charge before the enemy could fire, or to reload and prevent the enemy himself from launching a successful bayonet charge, or to fall back or regroup or bring in reserves. One had perhaps twenty seconds to make the decision, and the decision might have to be made again and again. Even so, the result of months of preparation was likely to turn upon a few minutes of actual fighting.

After the engagement had gone one way or the other, the senior officers had to go back to work, the unsuccessful to regroup, retreat, and try to reform an army at some safe distance, the successful to take prisoners and follow up their advantage. If the former failed and the latter did his job expeditiously and successfully, the losers had no option but to surrender, and the result was a clear-cut victory. Normally, however, the unsuccessful were likely to proceed frantically and the successful leisurely, with the result that the doings of the rival senior commanders canceled one another out. In that event the battle was more or less a draw, and the "winner" was he who had scored the greatest number of counters in the form of enemies killed, wounded, and captured.

The taking of prisoners, either directly in battle or as the result of a formal surrender, wants particular notice. The idea of taking prisoners (except for ransom or enslavement) was itself a polite convention, a long step toward civilized war. In the eighteenth century the convention was extended to elaborate lengths, and any man who violated the rules of capture forfeited all claims to honor, no matter how gallantly he may have behaved in battle. When a combatant surrendered, he was not only immune to further danger or harassment; he was also entitled to the same preferential or deferential treatment to which his rank and status entitled him at home. On the other hand, those who surrendered were honor-bound to behave in accordance with the terms of their capitulation. If a general surrendered, he was obliged to take his men home, and neither he nor they could participate in the war again unless they were exchanged for equivalent opposite numbers, rank for rank, captured by his country. Exchanges, it should be added, were often bookkeeping or scorekeeping transactions, not actual trades of live bodies; and captives in one war were eligible to participate in the next even if they had not been exchanged.

Individual captives were ordinarily "paroled," which is

to say released upon their honor; this meant not only that they were not to fight again unless exchanged, but also that they were to confine their movements to specified areas. In any war, thousands of paroled officers and men were to be found milling around near combat zones, able-bodied but inactivated, like so many hockey players in the penalty box. Thus during the American Revolutionary War, John Laurens, captured at the fall of Charleston, was paroled to the state of Pennsylvania. His sense of honor made the invisible state lines a prison as inescapable as the Tower of London, in which his father was physically confined. It not only prevented him, while awaiting exchange for a captured British colonel, from reentering the fighting; it also caused him to miss the wedding in New York of his friend Alexander Hamilton. Contrariwise, John André had to be executed after his capture on his subversive mission to West Point because he was out of uniform when caught; had the major been taken while doing exactly the same thing in proper attire, he would have been routinely paroled.

There were two main weaknesses in this charming eighteenth-century system of civilized war. One was that things never quite worked out in practice the way they were supposed to work as a gentlemanly ideal. In addition to the snafus that always prevent battles and campaigns from unfolding in accordance with textbook models, there were—it is our sad duty to record—no small number of cads and bounders around who winked at and sometimes actually, if surreptitiously, violated the rules. The second and more important weakness was that polite war was ill adapted for resolving the international conflicts that erupted in the last part of the century, since those sometimes entailed fighting with and against non-Europeans; and what was worse, it involved fighting with and against otherwise civilized nations who were succumbing to the then-endemic, soon to become pandemic, social malaise of democratization.

All this leads us to the War for American Independence. It was inherent in that conflict that it would be unsatisfactory to contemporary admirers of the military arts. In the first place, it was not a formal war between organized nation states, for the United States was not yet a real country. The burden of the fighting on the American side, in the initial phases, was carried by civilians, organized loosely into ill-disciplined militia units when they were organized at all. In addition, the Americans were fighting for a cause, which made them impatient with the niceties of the game. Moreover, there were, throughout the war, roving gangs of armed brigands on both sides, Patriot and Loyalist—such as the "Skinners" and "Cowboys" of upstate New York—who used the war as an excuse for random villainy.

Apart from such informal pickup groups, one can characterize the roster of participants in the conflict as being of five general, culturally distinct descriptions. One was the British armed forces, including the Hessian mercenaries, who were trained and disciplined in the ways of formal European war. A second was the New England militiamen, whose style of fighting was epitomized by their conduct in the fray at Lexington and Concord: they scarcely set records for bravery in their direct confrontations with the Redcoats and afterward hid behind rocks along the return route to Boston and shot the British dead. Equally characteristic of the Yankees was what the Connecticut militia did upon hearing the news of Lexington and Concord: twenty thousand militiamen gathered in a matter of hours and marched, not to Boston, but to upstate New York, with a view toward seizing control of land there. The more magnanimous British commanders viewed the Yankees as fiercely patriotic guerrillas; most, however, viewed them as murderers and thieves. American regulars subsequently came to regard them as undisciplined, cowardly provincials.

The third set of combatants, and the most important

to the American cause, was the evolving Continental regular force. In time the Continentals came to be the equal of the British in understanding the rules of the game and in having the courage and discipline required to play it, and they developed a toughness that probably made them the Redcoats' superiors as fighting men. But that development was slow in coming, and in the meantime the Continentals were a mixed bag. The long, painful process by which the enlisted men were forged into a disciplined army is well known. More interesting and more important for our present purposes are the American officers. Among these were a considerable number of experienced European officers who had volunteered for service in the American army, and one might have expected their presence to have imparted a certain tone. Actually, however, most of the European volunteers were adventurers, outcasts, misfits, or other persons with stains on their character: not gentlemen. We remember and justly celebrate the services rendered by Baron von Steuben, Thaddeus Kosciuszko, and the marquis de Lafayette; we sometimes forget that for every one of them there were ten of the likes of Philippe de Coudray, Charles Lee, Roche de Fermoy, Horatio Gates, and Thomas Conway.

As for the home-grown officers, they tended during the early part of the war to be either dilettantes or commanders whose experience had been in the most ungentlemanly business of fighting Indians. At the beginning, the main qualifications for obtaining commissions were political connections, social status, pretensions to being gentlemen (which included having read treatises on matters military), and independent means and a willingness to spend the same on raising and equipping one's men. Typical of the officers of this description was Philip Schuyler, who commanded the army of the northern department in New York. Schuyler has been unfairly maligned as an incompetent; in actuality he was able as a staff officer, being a gifted administrator and supply man, but he was hopeless as a field commander. It was not that he lacked courage or the ability to lead; rather, he was so polite and proper that he took forever to get his preparations just so. He and his British counterpart, "Gentleman Johnny" Burgoyne, might have continued their elaborate preliminary waltzing for years without ever engaging in battle, had not Schuyler been removed from command. Schuyler was truly in his element when playing the part of the magnanimous victor; his graciousness and hospitality in dealing with captured British officers were legendary in the British army. Unfortunately for all concerned, he did not often have the opportunity to play that role.

The fourth set of players was the frontiersmen. When we talk of frontiersmen, from the back country of Pennsylvania down through the Carolina piedmont, we are not talking about settlers of English extraction, but mainly of people of Celtic origins—Highland Scots, Welshmen, Cornishmen, and above all, Scotch-Irishmen. The Celts had always been outcasts in Europe, the progress of civilization having often passed them by; and though their American descendants had advanced so far as to put on clothes, they continued to be fierce, unrestrained, and sometimes savage warriors. In one sense they were in the European spirit: they did prove their manhood by their prowess and bravery in battle. But as was culturally characteristic of them, they carried the matter to extremes. They fought and killed for the sheer hellish joy of it; they asked for no quarter and gave none; they fought as regulars, as militiamen, and as virtually private armies, as the spirit moved them; they were superb soldiers whenever an enemy was nearby and troublemakers when no fighting was in the offing. They carried long rifles, which were so deadly as to spoil the game, and some frontiersmen were said to have taken up the Indian habit of scalping their enemies. The nadir of the Revolutionary War, at least from the point of view of war as a civilized game, came at Kings Mountain on October 7, 1780, when the adversaries on both sides happened to be men of Celtic extraction.

Finally, there were the Indians, who fought at times on the side of the British. The Indians afford a classic illustration of the distinction between warfare and war. They engaged in warfare, some of them almost incessantly, but never in war; every so-called Indian war from Pequot's to King Philip's to Pontiac's was by definition a misnomer. The idea that "war" was a separate thing from "peace," that it was illegitimate to slay one's tribal enemies in those intervals when no war was officially declared, was alien to their culture. So, too, was the idea that even during a state of intense hostilities, it was improper to kill enemy males who were not wearing some indication of their status as warriors, to kill prisoners, to butcher women and children, or to destroy civilian property. And as to weaponry, if the frontiersman's long rifle was impolite, the Indian's tomahawk was downright rude.

British attempts to reconcile a polite view of war with the use of Indians are pathetically yet comically illustrated by the charge that Burgoyne made to his Indian allies in 1777. "Warriors," he said to the assembled aborigines in his impeccable Johnsonian style, "go forth in the might of your valor and your cause; strike at the common enemies of Great Britain and America, disturbers of public order, peace and happiness, destroyers of commerce, parricides of the state." Continuing as if he thought his audience knew what he was talking about, he urged his allies "to regulate your passions when they overbear, to point out where it is nobler to spare than to revenge, to discriminate the degrees of guilt, to suspend the uplifted stroke, to chastise and not to destroy." He positively forbade the killing of "aged men, women, and children," and he insisted that "prisoners must be secure from the knife or hatchet even in the time of actual conflict." Magnanimously he allowed the taking of "the scalps of the dead when killed by your fire or in fair opposition," but he

warned that "on no account or pretence or subtlety or pre-
varication are they to be taken from the wounded or even
from the dying." It is reported that the guffaws of the Indians were echoed in the Houses of Parliament.

In light of all that has been said, one can understand
why the Revolutionary War was aesthetically a mixed bag.
To be sure, it had its flashes of brilliant strategy and tactics
and many episodes of gallantry and courage, such as
Hamilton's capture of Redoubt Number Ten at Yorktown.
Moreover, the war raised the cultural level of the tens of
thousands of young Americans who participated in it. Few
of the rank-and-file soldiers had ever attended the theater,
but during the war nearly every camp, as a means of keeping up morale, built stages on which plays by the most
fashionable authors were performed. Similarly, they were
introduced to good music: concerts featuring the music
of Haydn and Handel were repeatedly performed for them
by professional musicians. "Nothing is more agreeable,
and ornamental," wrote Washington, "than good music;
every officer, for the credit of his corps, should take care
to provide it." In addition, every camp had artists and
poets. Perhaps the most able poet was John Parke, a
colonel who whiled away the dreary hours at Valley Forge
by translating what would become the first edition of
Horace's *Odes* to be published in America. Of the artists,
Charles Wilson Peale was also at Valley Forge, where he
produced, among other works, portraits of more than forty
officers.

On the other hand, the war was frequently marked
by blundering, incompetence, treachery, and brutality, and
as in Gates's monumental flight from Camden, it sometimes degenerated into low comedy. The militiamen proved
cowardly in battle, whenever they showed enough discipline to wait around for a battle to start. (Regular officers
normally deployed them at the rear, so that when they
fled it would not dishearten the regulars. Morgan was an
exception; he is said to have put them at the front, with

the understanding that they might die at the hands of the British if they stood and fought but would certainly die at the hands of his riflemen if they did not.) As to the frontiersmen, they sometimes fought and sometimes did not. When they did, they were brave, but they were also brutal, disruptive, and prone to mutiny. (When one thinks of the largely Scotch-Irish Pennsylvania line, one can recall a few, but only a few, occasions when they distinguished themselves in combat. What more readily comes to mind is their mutiny in 1781 or the occasion two and a half years later when, drunk as lords, they marched around Independence Hall for several hours, poking muskets through windows at the terrified congressmen inside and demanding their back pay.) As to the Indians, mercifully they were used sparingly. When they were used, their conduct fell conspicuously short of Burgoyne's fastidious standards. (A single example, taken from Sullivan's report of his expedition to western New York in September, 1779, tells all. Thomas Boyd and another member of a scouting party had fallen into Indian hands. When the bodies were found, it was discovered that the prisoners had been subjected to "unparalleled tortures." The Indians "had whipped them in the most cruel manner, pulled out Mr. Boid's nails, cut off his nose, plucked out one of his eyes, cut out his tongue, stabbed him with spears . . . & inflicted other tortures which decency will not permit me to mention; lastly cut off his head.")

Nor was departure from honorable behavior confined to the irregulars. The British, for their part, often conducted themselves shamefully. To be sure, they might have taken the position that the Americans were rebels and therefore entitled to no further amenities than the hangman's rope. It is to their credit that they did not. But once they had committed themselves to regarding the Americans as rival soldiers, they were obliged to comport themselves accordingly, and this they did not always do. What Sir William Howe and Burgoyne did after the defeat at

Saratoga was scarcely Britain's finest hour. The terms under which Burgoyne surrendered to Gates stipulated that the captured British army march to a port, embark for England, and not serve again in America; as is well known, Howe sent a secret message to Burgoyne, saying that once Burgoyne got his men on transports in Boston, the Germans could be shipped to England, but the three thousand British troops were to be sent to New York for reassignment. Nor did the British bathe themselves in undying honor by suborning Benedict Arnold or by imprisoning captives in stinking hulks in Wallabout Bay and in the old sugarhouses of New York City. And then there was Banastre Tarleton, a man of passionate hatreds who contributed to the enrichment of the American language: the phrase "Tarleton's Quarter" was added to the lexicon to describe his practice of murdering captives.

Among the officers on the American side, some both distinguished themselves as soldiers and demonstrated that to say "an officer and a gentleman" is redundant. But these were the exceptional few: after Washington, Nathanael Green, and a handful of the Europeans, the ranks of the unblemished run out quickly. And even Washington was not always blameless. More than once his carping comments about his French allies were such that under other circumstances, they would have been sufficient to provoke duels, and he was quite willing to hang the innocent British prisoner, Charles Asgill, in retaliation against the unauthorized misbehavior of New York Loyalists.

And think of this. On a cold winter's night in 1776, when all proper gentlemen were ensconced for the season, Washington crept across the Delaware and successfully attacked, in their beds in Trenton, German mercenaries who were sleeping off the effects of their celebration of the nativity of Our Lord. This was Washington's only clear-cut victory in his six years as commander in chief before Yorktown.

Disillusionment was widespread, especially among

the more romantic and idealistic junior officers. The war-time correspondence of Washington's ablest aide-de-camp, young Alexander Hamilton, poignantly illustrates the disillusionment. Hamilton, as the illegitimate son of a no-good member of a very good Scottish family, was perhaps more sensitive than most, for he passionately wanted to believe that there were people who comported themselves honorably at all times; but otherwise he was not atypical. In 1776 Hamilton's naive enthusiasm was such that he expressed faith not only in the rich and well-born but even in the goodness and wisdom of the masses. By 1780 all the scales had been stripped from his eyes. "The authorized maxims and practices of war," he wrote, "are the satire of human nature. They countenance almost every species of seduction as well as violence; and the General that can make most traitors in the army of his adversary is frequently most applauded." Despairing, he declared that "the worst of evils seems to be coming upon us—*a loss of our virtue.* . . . I hate Congress—I hate the army—I hate the world—I hate myself. The whole is a mass of fools and knaves."

The point of all this is that the War for American Independence marked the end of an era and the beginning of a new age. Politically, the ringing of the Liberty Bell foretokened the impending demise of monarchy and the birth of republicanism and of republicanism's own fearsome progeny, democracy. We are accustomed to that idea. We tend to forget that along with monarchy the whole polite, genteel world symbolized by J. S. Bach and Thomas Chippendale, by formal gardens and minuets, died also. And not the least tragic of the casualties of that war was gentlemanly warfare itself.

It was not that the conception of war as a civilized, honorable game died a sudden death. Clearly, the ideal continued to live throughout the nineteenth century and into the twentieth, especially in the American South, where the related ideals of gentlemanly behavior and honorable conduct also survived. Indeed, serious reflection will show that the conception is still with us, albeit in diluted and vulgarized form. Consider, for instance, the popular and media protests during the Vietnamese conflict. Against a backdrop of prospective nuclear holocaust, amid vivid nightly telecasts of the carnage in that hellish jungle, what was it that was most fervently protested? That in its bombing raids, at My Lai, and in the crossing of the imaginary "out of bounds" line of Cambodia, the United States was not "playing fair."

Rather, the unfortunate fact is that civilized war, like many another sociocultural institution that was born in the hothouse environment of the eighteenth century, outlived the social and technological conditions that gave it birth. The ideal persisted, but reality progressively encroached upon it—through the Napoleonic wars, the Civil War, the trenches of World War I, Iwo Jima, Nagasaki, Korea, Vietnam—making it increasingly difficult and ultimately impossible to fight wars in a civilized fashion. As long as it survived as a game with rules, war exercised a beneficent effect upon human society—both by restraining random and socially destructive violence and by exalting man's nobler attributes. It is doubtful whether we can do without it; the symptoms of its demise are everywhere around us.

In Europe, the birth of the modern world—with all its hopes and all its horrors—is sometimes dated from the Battle of Valmy in 1792, when a band of ragged Frenchmen, inspired with the awesomely destructive ideals of liberté, egalité, and fraternité, turned back a Prussian army which, under the older and more polite rules of war, would have been invincible. But to date the end and the beginning at Valmy is to miss the real end-and-beginning by seventeen years. The shots fired at Lexington in 1775 are still being heard around the world: from that moment onward, there has been no turning back. God help us.

4

ON THE LATE
DISTURBANCES
IN MASSACHUSETTS

THE GENERAL OUTLINES OF THE EPISODE CALLED SHAYS'
rebellion are well known and well documented. During
the summer of 1786, town meetings in the five western-
most counties of Massachusetts sent delegates to extralegal
conventions, which drew up petitions of grievances to the
state legislature. Between August 29 and September 12,
mobs of armed horsemen, ranging in number from about
two hundred to about two thousand, prevented the sit-
ting of the Courts of Common Pleas in those counties
until such time as the legislature should act upon the
petitions. When the September session of the legislature adjourned without having acted, several thousand
malcontents, led by Daniel Shays and others, began to
drill and to form themselves into an insurgent army. The
state government and the Confederation Congress proved
unable to raise funds for suppressing the insurgents, but
enough money was raised by private subscriptions in
Boston and vicinity to equip a volunteer force of forty-
four hundred men. This force, under the command of
Benjamin Lincoln, marched westward in January. The
insurgents, lacking artillery and short on arms and am-
munition, tried to seize the Confederation arsenal at
Springfield before Lincoln could arrive, but their plans

miscarried. On January 25 they faced a force of loyal militiamen under William Shepard, who fired several rounds of grapeshot into their ranks at close range, killing four and wounding several others. The remainder fled. Lincoln and his army remained in the field for a time, capturing an occasional leader, and minor violence continued to flare for another six months; but the organized rebellion, such as it was, was over.[1]

The significance of the rebellion is likewise well known and well documented: it gave powerful stimulus to the movement toward the Constitutional Convention that met in Philadelphia in May. Only one historian has seriously argued that the convention would have materialized even if Shays' Rebellion had never happened, and his argument is not convincing.[2] Congress had declined to endorse the call for the Philadelphia Convention that had been issued by the Annapolis Convention. As accounts of the tumults in Massachusetts spread over the country, however, seven states responded by electing delegates anyway. Then, in early February, Congress received Governor James Bowdoin's official proclamation that a state of rebellion existed in Massachusetts. The proclamation, together with news that New York had killed the revenue amendment that had been pending since 1783, led Congress on February 21 to adopt the resolutions of the Annapolis Convention and to authorize the Philadelphia Convention. Five more states then chose delegates to the convention.[3]

But despite the consensus as to what happened and as to its importance, Shays' Rebellion is far from a closed book. The insurrection was purposefully misrepresented by some contemporaries, and it has been grossly misperceived by most modern historians. The contemporary misrepresentations reflected contemporary fears and hopes and led to the establishment of the Constitution. The misperceptions of historians reflect modern prejudices and lead nowhere.

LET US BEGIN WITH THE HISTORIANS. THE MORE OR LESS official interpretation is that compiled by Project 87 of the American Historical Association and the American Political Science Association for a Calendar of Commemorative Dates for the Bicentennial. Shays, we are told, was a "destitute farmer" who organized other "debt-ridden farmers" in a "rebellion against the Massachusetts government, which had failed to take action to assist the state's depressed farm population." David P. Szatmary, author of the most recent scholarly monograph on the subject, gives an added dimension to that interpretation, contending that the rebellion was "an economic conflict exacerbated by a cultural clash between a commercial society and a rural subsistence-oriented way of life."[4]

Szatmary also describes the "specific economic context" in which the rebellion supposedly arose. At the end of the War for Independence, he tells us, wholesalers in Boston and other New England seaboard towns imported large quantities of British manufactures, thus taking on a great burden of debts and draining the region of specie. The wholesalers sold the goods on credit to retail shopkeepers in the interior, who in turn sold them on credit to farmers. This "chain of debt" became unbreakable when the British closed their West Indies to American shipping, thus preventing the wholesale merchants from trading their way out of their deficits. The merchants accordingly sued the retailers, who sued the farmers: in 1785 and 1786 the courts were jammed by an enormous increase in suits for debts. It was to prevent the trial of such suits that the armed bands gathered to close the courts in 1786.[5]

That is not the way things were. It is true that merchants, especially in Boston—who, it is important to observe, were mainly novices in international trade, most of the leading colonial merchants having been banished as Loyalists[6]—greatly overimported in 1783 and 1784. But it was they who were the "desperate debtors" in the state, for the goods proved largely unsalable. What they owed their British creditors for the goods that, for the most part, remained on their shelves cannot be precisely known, but it was somewhere between £100,000 and £300,000 in 1786, and their creditors were pressing them hard for payment. By contrast, the total indebtedness in the Massachusetts back country was around £55,000.[7] Significantly, the fall 1786 session of the legislature, which was rigorously unsympathetic to the proto-Shaysites and which was dominated by the "merchant party," enacted a law suspending all suits for debts for a period of eight months—and that retarded the rebellion not one jot. The suspension was extended the next year. The merchants, owing much and being owed little, were obviously not seriously damaged by this debtor-relief legislation.[8]

As for the insurgents, a close analysis of two relevant sets of documents suggests that although there were desperate debtors among them, including Daniel Shays himself, they were as a group by no means a "debtor class." The first documents are lists of rebels. In January, 1787, the legislature provided that all persons who had borne arms against the state, except for a handful of designated leaders, could receive full pardons simply by taking an oath of allegiance to the Commonwealth of Massachusetts and its constitution. Few rebels laid down their weapons to take advantage of the offer, but after the insurrection had proved futile, about three-fifths of them did so, for they were still seeking to obtain through regular political channels what they had failed to obtain through force of arms. By the end of October, more than three thousand men had taken the oath. The records of the oath taking, housed in the Massachusetts Archives, include the signatures, the towns, and for about a third of the repentant Shaysites, their occupations. We have tallied the signers by towns, and it turns out that they were far from evenly distributed. Indeed, between two-thirds and three-quarters of these known rebels came from just 50 of the 179 towns in the five-county area. By contrast, in 69 of those towns there were no Shaysites, and in 20 others, fewer than 1 percent of the adult males were Shaysites.[9]

The second relevant documents are the state property evaluations for 1786, which include, among many other items, figures for indebtedness, town by town.[10] If the rebellion was a response to private indebtedness, there should be at least a rough correlation between the distribution of Shaysites and the distribution of debts. Before making the comparisons necessary to determine what correlation there was, however, a few words about the applicability of quantitative analysis to the subject are in order. In general terms, it must be recollected that eighteenth-century Americans, unlike modern Americans, did not often think numerically. As a consequence, though their compilations of figures—for example, in tax lists, property inventories, and tables of imports and exports—are precise in appearance, they are always inexact guides to the reality they purport to reflect or measure.

In more specific terms, the Massachusetts Tax Evaluations of 1786 are marked by several weaknesses. One is that there is both internal and external evidence that they contain many mistakes, though these should average themselves out somewhat in the kind of broadly based comparison we are about to undertake. Another is that the evaluations record the debts owed *to* inhabitants of the towns, not *by* the inhabitants. This problem, however, is also compensated for to a considerable extent: given the difficulties of transportation and the typical distance of ten or fifteen miles between town centers, it seems unlikely that many retailers in the interior towns extended credit to farmers in other towns. A third weakness is that the records are compiled for whole towns, most of which contained two hundred to five hundred families; they do not indicate anything about individuals. Ascertaining the property holdings and debts of particular rebels from these sources is therefore impossible.

Nevertheless, gross as the data are, if private indebtedness underlay Shays' Rebellion, the towns with the largest indicated debts should correspond roughly to those that produced the most rebels, and those with the smallest recorded debts should have produced the fewest rebels. The fact is, however, that there is no correlation whatsoever. If we classify as "rebellious" those towns in which more than 10 percent of the adult males bore arms against the state and as "nonrebellious" those towns in which fewer than 1 percent did so, we can make the following statements. In Middlesex County, the per-adult-male indebtedness in rebellious towns was just over one and one half pounds, that in nonrebellious towns just over two and a half pounds. (A pound, Massachusetts currency, was worth $3.33; a dollar was six shillings.) In Hampshire County the debts per adult male in rebellious towns was a bit over twelve shillings, in nonrebellious towns about eighteen shillings. In Worcester County the comparable figures are three and a half pounds in rebellious towns and two and three-quarters in nonrebellious towns; and in Berkshire they are about ten shillings in both rebellious and nonrebellious towns. Bristol did not produce enough insurgents to justify a comparison; debts per man there were about two and a half pounds. Debts in Essex, Suffolk, and Plymouth, which produced no Shaysites, ranged from four pounds to more than twelve pounds per man.

The lack of correlation is seen more vividly when one compares neighboring towns in which commercial conditions were similar but participation in the rebellion was different. For instance, Conway had twelve shops, indicating that farmers bought locally, and a per-poll indebtedness of fifteen shillings, and nearby Greenfield had nineteen shops and a per-poll debt of seventeen shillings; yet nearly a fifth of the men in Conway rose in rebellion and only 9 of the 280 men in Greenfield did so. Such patterns occurred again and again.

Unquestionably, a great increase in litigation for debts did take place during the mid 1780s, but the increase did not indicate that merchants and shopkeepers were suing farmers and laborers for nonpayment of accounts for goods purchased in 1783/84. To begin with, many of the suits had originally been filed during the 1770s and had been in suspension since then.[11] Other aspects of the cases are suggested by the thorough statistical study of litigation in Plymouth County made by the legal historian William E. Nelson for the period 1725 to 1825. Prior to the Revolution, members of the "upper classes" (those identified as esquires, gentlemen, and merchants) sued members of the "lower classes" (farmers, seamen, transportation workers, and laborers) 4.2 times more frequently than those below sued them. During the 1780s, members of the upper classes appeared as plaintiffs against lower-class defendants only 1.4 to 1.6 times more frequently than they were sued by the lower classes. In other words, a large part of the increase in litigation was the result of a substantial growth in actions brought by men of the lower classes against men of the upper classes.[12]

Moreover, there was a shift in the nature of suits for debt. During the prewar period, 75 percent of all private litigation was between individuals for the collection of debts. Only 15 percent of the indebtedness suits concerned collection of debts for goods purchased; the rest involved loans secured by notes or bonds. In the post-Revolutionary period, cases for debts fell from 75 percent to 59 percent of all civil litigation, and actions in cases on accounts fell from 15 percent to 9 percent of all debt suits.[13] Even after allowing for a small increase in total litigation in some towns, it appears that suits for nonpayment of debts for goods purchased were fewer after the Revolution than before.

Van Beck Hall has compiled some revealing figures on suits for debt during the 1780s. For one thing, Hall reports that the upsurge in such litigation began in 1782, which was a year before the Boston merchants began their reckless importation. (That is readily explicable: the courts in the interior had been closed throughout most of the war.) For another, suits for debts continued to increase through 1785 but actually declined in 1786, the year Shays' Rebellion began. Hall has not tallied the cases by towns; but the average number of cases for the recognizance of debts for the state as a whole during the three years 1784 through 1786 was upwards of forty per thousand adult males. The rate in Worcester County was one hundred per thousand, the highest in the state—which would mean that one man in ten was sued for debt in Worcester County during that three-year period, if no one was sued more than once, which is most unlikely.[14]

As we have no comparable figures from other states or other times, these statistics tell us almost nothing; but we can learn something by comparing the numbers of suits with the numbers of Shaysites. Hall tells us that about 600 suits for debt were being heard in Worcester County every year during the period. Szatmary tells us that the number of oath-taking insurgents was 969. That is not much of a correlation. And what does one do with Hampshire County? Hall says that the Court of Common Pleas heard 800 cases for debt in Hampshire County in 1785 alone. His source, however, indicates, not that 800 cases for debt were heard, but that 800 "civil cases" were heard. If it can be assumed that debt cases constituted roughly the same proportion of all civil cases in Hampshire County as in Plymouth, the number of debt cases would have been around 480 and the number of suits for debts for the purchase of goods less than 80. And yet in 1787, according to Szatmary, there were 1,427 oath-taking insurgents in Hampshire.[15]

The lack of correlation between suits for debts and rebelliousness appears more dramatically as one looks more closely. Hall found that one-tenth of the adult males in Worcester County were defendants in suits for recognizance of debts from 1784 through 1786; between one-twelfth and one-sixteenth of the adult males were oath-taking rebels. In Hampshire County only 1.6 percent of the adult males were defendants in such debt suits; yet 16.0 percent of the adult males bore arms against the state. Figures for individual towns in Hampshire make the discrepancy greater: in such towns as Colerain, Greenwich, Amherst, South Brimfield, New Salem, Pelham, Whatley, Ware, and Wendell, between two-fifths and two-thirds of the adult males took part in the uprising.[16] These oath takers were not mere sympathizers, mind you, but men who admitted to having borne arms against the state; the number who bore arms but for one reason or another did not take the oaths would swell the figures considerably. In other words, in the heart of Shays country, there were many times as many rebels as "desperate debtors."

One further point about debts: there was a considerable demand in the back country for an issue of paper money, which misled a few contemporaries and has almost uniformly misled historians into believing that private indebtedness was at the root of the troubles. But in five of the seven states that issued paper during the so-called paper-money movement of 1785–87 the primary purpose of the issue was to service public debts, and the main secondary purpose was to speculate in land. A small Georgia issue of 1786 was designed to help finance an expected Indian war. Only the South Carolina issue was designed for the relief of private debtors. What we are suggesting is that when half of the Massachusetts town petitions and all the county petitions called for paper money, it was generally understood that they were proposing to expunge, not private debts, but the state's public debts, as was being done by Rhode Island and, in less radical fashion, by New Jersey, New York, Pennsylvania, and North Carolina.[17]

Before considering the grievances and other forces that actually did bring on the rebellion, let us examine the extent to which the insurrection was a movement of farmers. Clearly the towns that produced most of the Shaysites were among those that Szatmary describes as "subsistence-oriented" and that Hall calls "the least commercial-cosmopolitan"—although, significantly, more towns of that description were nonrebellious than were rebellious. As noted earlier, about a third of the oath-taking rebels indicated their occupations. Szatmary has tallied these and found that 54 percent called themselves yeomen or husbandmen.[18] Our own count, conducted in a somewhat different way, yields a slightly higher figure. The point, however, is that the numbers of farmers were disproportionately low, inasmuch as farmers constituted 80 to almost 100 percent of the populations of the rebellious towns but only a little over 50 percent of the insurgents.

WHAT PRIMARILY INCITED THE REBELLION WAS, IN A word, taxation—a level of taxes that was not only unbearably heavy but also grossly unjust. Massachusetts, unlike the Congress and the other states, did not scale down its public debts to compensate for wartime fiscal dislocations and for depreciation of the currency, with the result that when the legislature consolidated them in the early 1780s, the state had a public debt of more than $5 million. Because the state government was slow and erratic in providing for its debts, the public paper circulated at a fraction of its face value, and most of it was bought by merchants in Boston and other eastern ports—the self-same new-rich merchants who were in such a deep hole because of overimporting unsalable British goods. The most endangered private debtors in Massachusetts, in other words, were precisely the people who were the greatest public creditors. When their British creditors began to put pressure on them, they in turn put pressure, not upon storekeepers in the interior, but upon the state government.[19]

Until 1785, violent opposition to tax collectors was only sporadic among inhabitants of the interior for the simple reason that most of them did not pay the taxes that were levied. Under the Massachusetts collection system, the state treasurer sent warrants to locally elected collectors through a cumbersome process that ultimately centered in the Courts of Common Pleas, but the perennial governor, John Hancock, had no interest in jeopardizing his great popularity by activating the process. The redemption of the public debt was scheduled to begin in 1785, however, and early in that year the public creditors began to demand increased taxes and the collection of those that were overdue. The legislature (in which the back country was greatly underrepresented, many of the interior towns having chosen to save money by not sending representatives) responded by enacting a stamp act in addition to the existing taxes. During the ensuing clamor, Governor Hancock announced that he was suffering a severe attack of gout—his gout was said to have been the best political barometer in the state—and declared that he would not stand for reelection. In his stead, in an election from which voters stayed away in droves, was chosen James Bowdoin, a Boston merchant, public creditor, and no-nonsense believer in the enforcement of laws. Under Bowdoin's prodding, the legislature began to enact a host of new taxes and to exert pressure for the collection of old taxes.[20]

Three details about Bowdoin's program are directly relevant. The first is sheer magnitude. In 1786 the legislature enacted new taxes amounting to about £3 per adult male in the three western counties—well over the average private indebtedness in Worcester and Hampshire and three times that in Berkshire. The combined load of overdue taxes and current taxes that were under execution in the three counties in 1787 was £286,265 (about £10 per adult male), as compared with a total private indebtedness of around £55,000 (less than £2 per adult male).[21] The taxes were more than the inhabitants could pay in a year or, indeed, in a decade. In fact, they were never paid, for in 1790 the federal government assumed Massachusetts' debts. That might help to explain why western Massachusetts, despite its political radicalism and its relatively noncommercial way of life, remained a stronghold of Hamiltonian federalism long after federalism was defunct elsewhere.

The second relevant point is that the burden of taxes was regressive. Only about 10 percent of the taxes levied and collected during the period 1781–86 came from import duties and excises, which fell on people who were most able to pay. The remaining 90 percent was direct taxes on property (land bore a disproportionate share) and on individuals. The latter, poll taxes, constituted about a third of the total and was payable by every male sixteen years of age and older, whether he had any property or not. Common laborers, who bore the heaviest burden in relation to their ability to pay, were ripe for rebellion if leadership were forthcoming; and it is revealing that in the lists of oath-taking insurgents, laborers are present far out of proportion to their numbers.[22]

Leadership was forthcoming as a consequence of the third relevant detail. Toward the end of the war, Massachusetts had issued certificates to compensate its continental soldiers for the depreciation of their pay, thereby increasing the state's debts by nearly $1 million. These certificates were scheduled to be redeemed in three annual specie payments beginning in January, 1784, but no payments had been made during the governorship of John Hancock. The veterans, most of whom had neglected their personal affairs during the war, were unable to wait for their compensation; by 1785 most of them had long since sold their certificates, commonly at about 2s. 6d. on the pound, or one-eighth of face value. Then the Bowdoin administration began to pay interest on the securities in specie and in 1786 began to redeem the principal, which involved a bit of arithmetic that the veterans found especially galling. A soldier who had had £100 in securities at the time of his discharge would have received perhaps £12.6s. in cash for them, and by 1786 he was being taxed to pay £6 a year in interest on them and £12 a year for retiring the principal. Bowdoin's pious words about public faith and credit were pure hypocrisy in the eyes of these men; and they were men who were accustomed to taking up arms in defense of their rights.[23]

These were highly flammable ingredients, and there were more. Ignorance was an important contributing factor, as was its enterprising companion, rumor. The state government made almost no efforts to inform back-country inhabitants about its problems, needs, intentions, or actions until the rebellion was well under way. During the summer of 1786, for example, the legislature passed an act making taxes payable in depreciated public securities, which would have greatly reduced the cash cost of the taxes, but this did not become generally known in the hinterlands.[24] Too, the back-countrymen had long been suspicious of and hostile toward the state government, especially its most visible manifestation, the courts; indeed, their resistance had virtually prevented government from functioning in the western counties since 1776. And perhaps most important was the legacy of the Revolution itself. The War for Independence had been fought over the principle of no taxation without representation, or so the Patriots in Boston had insisted; and the Declaration of Independence had proclaimed the natural right of the people to alter or abolish oppressive governments. Taxes levied by the state were now many, many times as oppressive as those that had been levied by the British, and the propertyless payers of poll taxes were no more represented in the Massachusetts General Court than Bostonians had been in Parliament. Finally, the former officers who provided most of the Shaysite leadership had been hailed as patriots and heroes when they had taken up arms against government in 1776, and it should scarcely be surprising if they believed that the same ought to be the case in 1786.

WE HAVE SLID BY DEGREES INTO THE NEXT ASPECT OF the topic, perceptions of the rebellion by contemporaries. At first there was no confusion at all about the sources of the uprising, at least among people on the scene in the interior of Massachusetts. The Reverend Bezaleel Howard of Springfield, who penned a lengthy running account of events, recorded that "the Commotions and Disturbances took their rise from the venality and Exorbitant Demand of the Genl. Court in Taxation and their appropriating of the Impost & Excise for the payment of the Intrest of the soldiers notes, which was sold for 2/6 on the pound." He cited as a secondary cause general hostility toward courts and lawyers and the outlandish fees that were being charged by judges and attorneys.[25] John Adams, who was kept well informed by friends at home even though he was in London, wrote to Jefferson: "Don't be allarmed at the late Turbulence in New England. The Massachusetts Assembly had, in its Zeal to get the better of their Debt, laid on a Tax, rather heavier than the People could bear; but all will be well."[26] George Richards Minot, in the first published history of the insurrection (1788), singled out the same grievances that the Reverend Howard had identified.[27]

One man—Superintendent of War Henry Knox—who understood the tumults the same way that Howard, Adams, and Minot did, nonetheless chose for political reasons to fabricate a different explanation. A steady stream of correspondence supplied Knox with eyewitness information, and he went to Massachusetts for a personal inspection; but nothing he learned squared with what he wrote to his old comrade in arms George Washington. "That taxes may be the ostensible cause is true," wrote Knox, "but that they are the true cause is as far remote from truth as light from darkness." What the insurgents were really seeking was "a common division of property, annihilation of all debts both public and private, and to have agrarian laws and unfounded paper money." More than a fifth of the men in several populous counties were under arms, Knox went on, and together with others from Rhode Island, Connecticut, and New Hampshire, they already numbered "12 or 15,000 desperate and unprincipled men," and their ranks were swelling daily. If they succeeded, they would soon be marching westward and southward, spreading anarchy and bloodshed the length and breadth of the land. This letter, in one form and another, found its way into newspapers and was circulated widely in private correspondence. It was the nearly hysterical reaction to this version of Shays' Rebellion that so powerfully stimulated the movement for a Constitutional Convention—just as Knox, and ardent nationalist, hoped it might.[28]

In considering the way the nation responded to Knox's deception, it is useful to recall two features of the perceptual apparatus that characterized public discourse among eighteenth-century Americans. The first was the habit of believing in conspiracies. In 1776 it had not been only quasi-paranoid ideologues who had believed that the British ministry harbored designs to enslave America; such sober-minded Patriots as Washington and Dickinson were similarly deluded. Nor did the habit die with independence. The establishment in 1783 of the Society of the Cincinnati as a fraternal order of former army officers was widely regarded as a plot to establish a hereditary aristocracy. In 1785, Massachusetts congressmen refused to respect the instructions of the state legislature to seek a general convention to enlarge the powers of Congress on the ground that "plans have been artfully laid, and vigorously pursued," to change "our republican Governments, into baleful Aristocracies." In 1787, rumors of a plot to establish a monarchy were widely believed. Soon afterward, Federalists would be convinced that Jeffersonian Republicans were secret Jacobins, and the Republicans would be equally convinced that Hamiltonians were secret monarchists.[29]

The second was the pervasiveness of the classical revival and what ancient history taught about the fragility of republics. Americans were acutely aware of the life cycle of republics, in which manly virtue gave way to effeminacy and vice, republican liberty to licentiousness; then licentiousness degenerated into anarchy, and anarchy gave way to tyranny. Always, Catilines, Sullas, and Caesars, driven by ambition and avarice, stood ready to rouse the multitudes and destroy the republic. This awareness, along with the complementary preoccupation with conspiracies, conditioned the way in which most Americans reacted to the tumults in Massachusetts.[30]

One other common belief, that the rebellion was instigated or infiltrated and taken over by Tories or the British, was likewise probably unfounded. It cannot, however, be dismissed out of hand. Rumors abounded. Thomas Clarke wrote to Bowdoin early in September that two Tory physicians, among others, were circulating papers whose purport was "in plain terms—A Petition to the Parliament of Great Britain." Bowdoin ask Artemus Ward to investigate; Ward replied that the disturbances were the work of "British emissaries" who had engaged about a dozen men to ride through the countryside and "stimulate the unwary to acts of disorder & violence." Ward added a suspicion, entertained by many, that Sir Guy Carlton, Lord Dorchester, who had recently arrived as governor of Canada, had sinister designs. The Virginia congressman Edward Carrington wrote from New York that Dorchester was in contact with the insurgents; and in mid January, General Shepard wrote to Bowdoin that he had seen two British emissaries among the insurgents.[31]

A group of insurgents in Worcester had resolved on December 7 that they "despise the Idea of being Instigated by british Emissaries which is so streniously Propigated by the Enemies of our Liberties."[32] This resolution doubtless expressed the sentiments of the vast majority of Shaysites, and yet the rumors were not entirely devoid of substance. There is hard evidence that a number of Tories, all of whom were physicians, were actively fomenting unrest; among them were John Hulburt of Alford (Berkshire County), James Freeland of Sutton (Worcester), Samuel Williard of Uxbridge (Worcester), Marshall Spring of Watertown (Middlesex), and Samuel Kittridge of Groton (Middlesex).[33] Another letter suggests that Tories were taking over the insurrection, whether the insurgents were aware of it or not. On November 6 Samuel Holden Parsons wrote to Knox of eyewitness evidence that Shaysites, two or three thousand strong, were drilling and practicing maneuvers daily, "& that they were punctually paid 3/ in Cash each day they are employed in this Business . . . the fire is kindled from Causes we are not fully informed of."[34] We have seen no evidence that supports Parson's statement; but it is interesting that late in February, Lord Dorchester himself added a cryptic postscript to a letter from Canada: "Mr. Shays, who headed the Massachusetts insurgents, arrived in this province the 24th with four of his officers."[35] Wherever the insurgents got the money to finance their operations, they got a surprising amount of it.

FINALLY, LET US END AS WE BEGAN, WITH THE ACCOUNTS of historians. Because the political usefulness of Knox's fabricated version had passed, that version was substantially forgotten for almost a century after the adoption of the Constitution, and historians faithfully reported that public debts, taxes, and hostility to courts had prompted the rising. As indicated, Minot treated the subject in that manner, as did Mercy Warren in her *History of Massachusetts* (1805), John Marshall in his five-volume *Life of George Washington* (1804–7), and Richard Hildreth in his monumental six-volume *History of the United States* (1849–52).

Then occurred a casebook example of the rewriting of history to make it accord with current preoccupations and values. In the late 1870s Edward Bellamy (who would gain international attention a decade later with his industrial utopian novel, *Looking Backward*) was working as a journalist in his native Berkshire County, Massachusetts. His ever-sensitive social conscience had him troubled about agrarian unrest in the West; this was the age of the Granger Movement and the Greenback Movement and was a time of severe agricultural as well as industrial depression. In that context, Bellamy wrote and published serially in a Great Barrington newspaper, the *Berkshire Courier*, a novel called *The Duke of Stockbridge: A Romance of Shays' Rebellion*, in which he depicted the rebels sympathetically as a band of embattled farmers, oppressed by and deeply indebted to an avaricious and heartless merchant class. The novel was not published in book form until 1900, by which time Bellamy's renown in leftist and reform circles ensured it a large readership. Meanwhile, John Fiske, in his popular book *The Critical Period of American History* (1888), had likewise depicted the rebellion as an uprising of debtor-farmers, though he included taxes and lawyers among their complaints. This he did despite the fact that the only primary sources supporting the debtor-farmer interpretation were the false charges made by Bowdoin and his supporters in a deliberate effort to discredit the insurgents and shift the odium from themselves. During the next two decades—during, that is, the Populist and Progressive periods, when contemporary problems were increasingly perceived in terms of economic class struggles—the farmer-debtor interpretation came to be unquestioningly accepted by historians. It has continued to prevail ever since.

But now that most Americans, or at least most of them outside the Washington, D.C., metropolitan area, have come once again to realize that the greatest danger to their liberties arises from excessively large and expensive government, perhaps the time has arrived for scrapping an interpretation that reflects the rhetoric of populism and for returning to one that reflects the realities of the "late Disturbances in Massachusetts."

NOTES

1. George Richards Minot, *The History of the Insurrections, in Massachusetts* (Worcester, Mass., 1788), was the first and is still a classic work on the subject. The standard authorities are Robert J. Taylor's *Western Massachusetts in the Revolution* (Providence, R.I., 1954) and Marion L. Starkey's *A Little Rebellion* (New York, 1955). A great deal of supplementary information is contained in Van Beck Hall's *Politics without Parties: Massachusetts, 1780-1791* (Pittsburgh, Pa., 1972). The most recent scholarly study is David P. Szatmary's *Shays' Rebellion: The Making of an Agrarian Insurrection* (Amherst, Mass., 1980). See also Barbara Karsky, "Agrarian Radicalism in the Late Revolutionary Period (1780-1795)," in *New Wine in Old Skins: A Comparative View of Socio-Political Structures and Values Affecting the American Revolution*, ed. Erich Angermann et al. (Stuttgart, 1976), pp. 87-114. The most important collection of primary sources on the rebellion is in the Massachusetts Archives; other important collections are in the Massachusetts Historical Society and the American Antiquarian Society. Most of what follows is derived from study of those three collections.

2. Robert A. Feer, "Shays's Rebellion and the Constitution: A Study in Causation," *New England Quarterly* 42 (Sept. 1969): 388-410.

3. The interplay between news of the rebellion and the actions of Congress and the states is detailed in Forrest McDonald, *E Pluribus Unum: The Formation of the American Republic, 1776-1790* (Indianapolis, Ind., 1979), pp. 244-56.

4. Szatmary, *Shays' Rebellion*, p. 18.

5. Ibid., chaps. 2 and 3 passim. Note that on page 60 Szatmary says, "No wholesaler or retailer admitted to involvement in the uprising," yet Trulove Brewster in the town of Adams designated himself "merchant" in signing the loyalty oath. The nature of the records is such as to render suspect any exact or categoric statements based upon them.

6. Probably three-fourths or more of the mercantile community of Boston was banished. "An Act to prevent the return to this state of certain persons therein named," published in the *Boston Gazette* for Sept. 1, 1783, lists 54 persons as merchants,

18 as mariners, 11 as traders, and 4 as shopkeepers. Another 66 were called Esquire, perhaps half of these being merchants, since royal officials and country gentlemen were listed separately as such. About 150 merchants were active in Boston after the war, nor more than 20 of whom had been active as merchants before the war.

7. That the Bostonians greatly overimported in 1783/84 is abundantly evident; see, e.g., advertisements in Boston newspapers, 1783–85; James B. Hedges, *The Browns of Providence Plantations: Colonial Years* (Cambridge, Mass., 1952), p. 288; Jacob Sebor to Silas Deane, Nov. 10, 1784, in *Correspondence between Silas Deane, His Brothers, and Their Business and Political Associates, 1771–1795* (Hartford, Conn., 1930), p. 201; Moses Brown to Champion and Dickason, June 26, 1785, in Moses Brown Papers, Rhode Island Historical Society; *General Evening Post*, (London) Aug. 19–21, 1783; Warren to Adams, June 24 and Oct. 27, 1783, in Massachusetts Historical Society, *Warren-Adams Letters*, vol 2: *1778–1814* (Boston, Mass., 1925), pp. 219, 232; Higginson to Adams, Aug. 8, 1785, in "Higginson Letters," ed. J. Franklin Jameson, American Historical Association *Annual Report* I (1896): 723. For evidence that the Boston merchants were unable to sell the imported goods and were, as debtors, in a desperate plight by 1785, see, e.g., Moses Brown to Champion and Dickason, June 26, 1785, as cited above, which states flatly that this was the case; Christian Febiger to J. Sobotken, June 15, 1785, in *Magazine of American History* (1882): 352, in which a Danish mercantile agent reports that the Boston merchants had "an amazing Superfluity of all kinds of European goods" because "they have no Back Country to consume their Goods"; the manuscript volume *Evaluation and Taxes*, 1786, vol. 163, in the Massachusetts Archives; James Swan's *National Arithmetick* (Boston, Mass., 1786), pp. 25, 82, indicating that Boston merchants had been able to pay for much of their imported goods with war-accumulated specie, but still owed well over £100,000; William B. Weeden's reference to the papers of the Boston firm of Amory and Amory in his *Economic and Social History of New England, 1620–1789*, 2 vols. (New York, 1890), 2:819, showing that that house was proving unable, as early as 1784, to sell the English goods it had imported; the advertisements in the *Massachusetts Spy* (Worcester), Jan. 5, 1786, showing attempts of Boston mer-

chants to sell British goods; the Christopher Gore Papers, Baker Library, Harvard, showing the efforts of a Boston merchant, hired by the London firm of Champion and Dickason, to collect debts owed by Boston merchants; and "A Return of Excise and Dutied Articles Which Were on Hand or Brought into the Several Towns Herewith Annexed," in the Sedgwick Papers, Massachusetts Historical Society, indicating the general volume of trade in Berkshire County—fifty-nine purchases of outside goods in two years, 1788–90, totaling only about $5,200 and none of the transactions being with Boston. The total amount of debts owed by Bostonians to London firms that was not supported by sales on credit to Massachusetts consumers cannot be reckoned. James B. Hedges estimated that the amount was between £200,000 and £300,000.

8. *Acts and Laws of the Commonwealth of Massachusetts, 1780–1797*, 11 vols. (Boston, Mass., 1890–97), 4:113–16. Although the act did not especially harm the Boston merchants, it did not especially help them either, for debts due to the Massachusetts Bank and to British creditors were specifically exempted from the suspension.

9. Shays' Rebellion Papers, vol. 190, pp. 67–226, contains the oath takings.

10. Data on debts are in vol. 163, *Evaluation and Taxes*, 1786.

11. Szatmary, *Shays' Rebellion*, p. 30. Szatmary's evidence indicates that most of the suits for debts in western Massachusetts were brought by retailers, but he provides no data on who was being sued. Moreover, though he cites evidence of suits against retailers by wholesalers in Hampshire County, the only wholesaler-creditors he specifically mentions were from Connecticut, not Boston. People in central Massachusetts did very little trading with Boston, and those in the west did almost none.

12. William E. Nelson, *Dispute and Conflict Resolution in Plymouth County, Massachusetts, 1725–1825* (Chapel Hill, N.C., 1981), pp. 79–83.

13. Ibid., pp. 23–24, 159 n. 64.

14. Hall, *Politics without Parties*, pp. 192–93; full statistics by years for the five western counties are in table 47, p. 195. Recognizance cases were a means whereby a debtor could throw upon the creditor the burden and cost of an appeal to the state's

supreme court. If judgment were against the debtor, he could and usually did appeal the decision and then fail to continue the case in the higher court. In order to get the supreme court to affirm the judgment of the lower court, the creditor then had to file a recognizance. Shays himself was sued for debt twice in 1784—once for a £12 debt and a few months later for a £3 debt; Szatmary, *Shays' Rebellion*, p. 66.

15. Hall, *Politics without Parties*, pp. 192–93 and n.2; Taylor, *Western Massachusetts*, p. 127; Szatmary, *Shays' Rebellion*, p. 59. Our own count shows 717 oath takers in Worcester and 1,648 in Hampshire.

16. We have refrained from citing precise figures except when quoting other scholars, because precision is impossible, given the sources. Szatmary has reckoned as being in Worcester County a number of towns that were actually in Hampshire, but the results are more or less the same with either tally. Percentages are especially slippery because of the ambiguity about the number of polls recorded in the 1786 *Evaluation and Taxes*. Three figures are recorded: "rateable polls," "non-rateable polls" (sometimes described as "not supported by the town"), and sometimes "supported by the town"; Szatmary apparently used only the first figure. The recorders usually added the first two together to arrive at a total and did not count the third. Sometimes the figure ½ is recorded; what constituted half a poll is beyond our capacity to discern.

17. For analysis of the various issues of paper money see McDonald, *E Pluribus Unum*, pp. 80, 97–98, 111–12, 146–48, 179–80; and Forrest McDonald, *We the People: The Economic Origins of the Constitution* (Chicago, 1958), pp. 132, 326–39. For a concise contemporary account of what the Massachusetts paper would have been used for see Charles Pettit to Benjamin Franklin, Oct. 18, 1786, in Edmund C. Burnett, ed., *Letters of Members of the Continental Congress*, 8 vols. (Gloucester, Mass., 1963), 8:487: "They propose to reliquidate the public Debts and then pay them off in a Paper Money to be created without Funds."

18. Szatmary, *Shays' Rebellion*, p. 60.

19. Acts and Laws of Massachusetts, 1784, chap.25; Journal of the House of Representatives of the General Court of Massachusetts, Massachusetts Archives, Feb. 20 and June 8, 1784: *Massachusetts Centinel* (Boston), Sept. 21, 1785, and Feb. 8, 1786.

Good secondary accounts are in Merrill Jensen, *The New Nation* (New York, 1950), pp. 308–9; and E. James Ferguson, *The Power of the Purse: A History of American Public Finance, 1776–1790* (Chapel Hill, N.C., 1961), pp. 245–50.

20. Regarding violence in the early 1780s see Taylor, *Western Massachusetts*, pp. 103–27; Hall, *Politics without Parties*, pp. 185–89; and Pauline Maier, "Popular Uprisings and Civil Authority in Eighteenth-Century America," *William and Mary Quarterly* 27 (Jan., 1970): 4–35. The observations about the governorships of Hancock and Bowdoin are based largely on the Journal of the House of Representatives and the newspapers, especially, for Essex and Suffolk, *The Salem Mercury: Political, Commercial and Moral*; for Boston, *The Massachusetts Centinel* and *The Boston Gazette, and the Country Journal*; and for Newburyport, *The Essex Journal and the New-Hampshire Packet*. See also Bowdoin's messages to the legislature as recorded in the Journal of the House, especially messages of May 31, 1785, Feb. 20, June 2, and Nov. 3, 1786.

21. The figures are extrapolated from statistics in Hall, *Politics without Parties*, table 47, p. 195.

22. We have not seen, in either primary or secondary sources, a figure for the amount of excise taxes and imposts that were collected. Hall, in *Politics without Parties*, p. 97, says that the total of direct taxes *levied* from 1781 through 1786 was £1.4 million ($4,662,000), of which a third was in poll taxes. Ferguson, in *Power of the Purse*, p. 246, says that the arrears in 1786 were $931,000; subtracting that from the amount levied leaves $3,731,000 in direct taxes collected. The total taxes collected, according to Ferguson, was $4,159,000; subtracting the collected direct taxes from this leaves $428,000 for imposts and excise taxes, or just over 10 percent of the total.

23. *Hampshire Gazette*, Nov. 1 and 8, 1786; Shays' Rebellion Papers, Massachusetts Archives, vol. 189, pp. 75ff., 81–82, 83–84, 100, 171–72, 369–74, vol. 190, pp. 150, 238, 297; Sidney Kaplan, "Veteran Officers and Politics in Massachusetts, 1783–1787," *William and Mary Quarterly* 9 (1952): 29–57; Ferguson, *Power of the Purse*, pp. 247–48; Taylor, *Western Massachusetts*, pp. 130–32; Szatmary, *Shays' Rebellion*, pp. 64–65.

24. Taylor, *Western Massachusetts*, p. 129; *Massachusetts Centinel*, July 12, Aug. 26 and 30, Sept. 13, and Nov. 5, 1786; *Hamp-*

shire Herald (Springfield), Sept. 5 and 12, 1786; Acts and Laws, 1786.

25. Richard D. Brown, ed., "Shays' Rebellion and Its Aftermath: A View from Springfield, Massachusetts, 1787," *William and Mary Quarterly* 40 (1983): 598–615; the quotation is at p. 603. Interestingly, as early as Aug. 16, 1786, Timothy Bloodworth had written to the governor of North Carolina: "It appears there is some commotions in the Massachusetts about the Gentlemen of the longrobe, which order the populous wish to destroy"; Burnett, *Letters*, 8:434.

26. Adams to Jefferson, Nov. 30, 1786, in *The Adams-Jefferson Letters*, ed. Lester J. Cappon (Chapel Hill, N.C., 1959), p. 156.

27. See the opening chapter of Minot's *History of the Insurrections*. See also, e.g., Hamilton's assessment of the causes contained in his "Defence of the Funding System," July, 1795, in *The Papers of Alexander Hamilton*, ed. Harold C. Syrett et al., 26 vols. (New York, 1961–79), 19:18.

28. Knox to Joseph Williams, Oct. 16, 1786, to Congress, Oct. 18, 1786, to Washington, Oct. 23, 1786, James Swan to Knox, Oct. 26, 1786, Major North to Knox, Oct. 29, 1786—all in the Knox Papers, Massachusetts Historical Society; Edmund C. Burnett, *The Continental Congress* (New York, 1941), pp. 671–72; *Journals of the Continental Congress, 1774–1789*, ed. W. C. Ford et al., 34 vols. (Washington, D.C., 1904–37), Oct. 21, 1786. Examples can be seen in private correspondence as well as in newspapers. Abigail Adams, in London, wrote to Jefferson, mentioning the cry of some Shaysites for "an equal distribution of property," but she saw "Luxery and extravagance" as the causes of "these commotions"; *The Papers of Thomas Jefferson*, ed. Julian P. Boyd et al. (Princeton, N.J., 1950–), vol. 11, p. 86. Madison also wrote to his father that "an abolition of debts public & private, and a new division of property are strongly suspected to be in contemplation"; *The Papers of James Madison*, ed. Robert A. Rutland et al. (Chicago, 1962–), vol. 9, p. 154. That Washington believed Knox and accepted the agrarian-law implications is evident in his letters; see, e.g., Washington to Madison, Nov. 5, 1786, ibid., p. 161.

29. Barnard M. Bailyn, *The Ideological Origins of the American Revolution* (Cambridge, Mass., 1967), pp. 119–25; Gordon S. Wood, "Conspiracy and the Paranoid Style: Causality and

Deceit in the Eighteenth Century," *William and Mary Quarterly* 39 (July, 1982): 401–41. The quotation of the Massachusetts congressmen is from their letter to James Bowdoin, Sept. 3, 1785, in Burnett, *Letters*, 8:208. For an example of the credence given to rumors about monarchy see David Humphreys to Alexander Hamilton, Sept. 1, 1787, in *The Papers of Alexander Hamilton*, 4:241–42.

30. Regarding classical republicanism in America see Forrest McDonald, *Novus Ordo Seclorum: The Intellectual Origins of the Constitution* (Lawrence, Kans., 1985), pp. 66–77, and the sources cited therein.

31. Clarke to Bowdoin, Sept. 8, Ward to Bowdoin, Sept. 12, 1786, Shays' Rebellion Papers, vol. 190, pp. 238, 249–51, 253–61; Taylor, *Western Massachusetts*, pp. 149–50. See also a letter in the *Massachusetts Centinel*, May 19, 1787, in John P. Kaminski and Gaspare J. Saladino, eds., *The Documentary History of the Ratification of the Constitution*, vol. 13: *Commentaries on the Constitution, Public and Private*, vol. 1 (Madison, Wis., 1981), pp. 94–95, 96 n.

32. Shays' Rebellion Papers, vol. 190, pp. 297–98.

33. Ibid., vol. 189, pp. 75, 83–84, 100ff., 171–82, 369–74; *Massachusetts Centinel*, Dec. 13, 1786, Jan. 27 and May 16, 1787.

34. Parsons to Knox, Nov. 6, 1786, in Knox Papers, Massachusetts Archives.

35. Quoted in Starkey, *A Little Rebellion*, p. 166.

5

JOHN DICKINSON
AND THE CONSTITUTION

HAVING STUDIED EIGHTEENTH-CENTURY AMERICA ALL
our adult lives, we are prepared to offer a generalization:
the more one learns about the subject, the less prone one
becomes to make categorical statements. Who were the
first to resist British encroachments upon American liberties? who were the most important figures in bringing
about independence? what were the causes of independence? what did the Framers of the Constitution intend?
and hosts of lesser questions can be answered only, if they
can be answered at all, with a great many qualifications.
Indeed, when we read or hear a discourse upon any aspect of eighteenth-century America, our almost invariable
reaction is, "It was more complicated than that."

Nonetheless, there are a few exceptions. We would
hold, for example, that one man, and one alone, was indispensable to the American founding: George Washington. Similarly, we would argue that in the absence of about
eight delegates from Connecticut, Delaware, and the Carolinas, James Madison and James Wilson would have prevailed in the Federal Convention and that the resulting
constitution would not have been ratified. And once
the Constitution had been written and approved, the
man who was most responsible for the establishment

of a viable, durable government under it was Alexander Hamilton.

We would also insist—and shall attempt to show—that the most underrated of all the Founders of this nation was John Dickinson. Dickinson's standing in the American pantheon is shamefully obscure in view of his contributions toward the establishment of an independent regime of limited government, federalism, and liberty under law. His rendering of the Biblical definition of liberty, quoted earlier, is our favorite: "They should sit *every man* under his vine, and under his fig-tree, and NONE SHOULD MAKE THEM AFRAID." Few men labored as effectively as he did to bring that desideratum to pass.

DICKINSON WAS BORN IN MARYLAND IN 1732, THE SAME year as George Washington, but he grew up in Kent County, Delaware. His father, a wealthy tobacco planter, was a defector from the Society of Friends. John, like his father, refused to attend Quaker meetings, but he was nonetheless a devout Christian with strong Quaker leanings. At eighteen, after having received through private tutors a thorough education in Latin, ancient and modern history, and mathematics, he went to Philadelphia to read law with John Moland, an eminent attorney. Then he was sent to London to study law at the Middle Temple of the Inns of Court. Unlike many a young man with ample means, unsupervised in the most exciting city in the world, he really did study. Upon his return after three years, he was almost awesomely learned.

Dickinson quickly became a great success at the Pennsylvania bar, and not long afterward he succumbed to the lure of politics—the occupational hazard inherent among lawyers in a representative government. In 1760 he was elected to the Assembly of Delaware, and two years later he was elected to the legislature of Pennsylvania (until the Revolution, Delaware and Pennsylvania were not entirely separate; they shared the same governors but had different legislatures). During the next three decades, Dickinson practiced law in Pennsylvania, maintained an estate in Delaware, and was active in the politics of both.

His first important stand in Pennsylvania politics was characteristic of the way he would act throughout his career. In 1764 Benjamin Franklin and Joseph Galloway were conniving to have the Penn family's proprietary charter revoked and thus to change Pennsylvania into a royal colony. The colonists had genuine grievances, and revocation became a popular cause. But Dickinson was too steeped in British history to believe that kings and their agents were men of unalloyed virtue, and besides, he was instinctively wary of any sudden, irreversible actions. Accordingly, he fought Franklin and Galloway vigorously, arguing that, bad as the proprietors were, the charter did guarantee certain liberties, and Pennsylvanians could not trust the king or his ministers to improve their lot. Dickinson's position brought him unpopularity for a short time, but soon he proved to be a prophet. In 1765 George Grenville's ministry produced the Stamp Act, and worse measures were to follow.

In these circumstances, Dickinson rose to become the universally acknowledged leader of the American resistance, as the events of the next decade placed his particular combination of attitudes and abilities at a premium. For centuries, Englishmen had justified espousal or opposition to changes in the political order by insisting that they were seeking only to restore or preserve the traditional scheme of things. Now, in the imperial crisis of 1765–76, Americans needed a spokesman who could justify resistance to British authority in the same manner. They needed someone who could demonstrate that king and Parliament were making radical innovations and that the Americans were defending ancient traditions and rights. This was precisely the way Dickinson saw things, and few colonists could match his capacity to explain the position.

As a writer, he was masterful. As an orator, he was adjudged by John Adams (who disliked him) to be the equal of Patrick Henry, and there could be no higher praise than that.

The quantity, quality, and circulation of Dickinson's writings on behalf of the American cause surpassed those of any others. In 1765 he wrote the resolutions of the Stamp Act Congress, insisting that Britain had no right to tax the colonies. In 1767 he took up his pen to compose his most celebrated tract, the *Letters from a Farmer in Pennsylvania*, written in opposition to the Quartering Act, the Townshend Duties, and the Declaratory Act. The first of these acts required the colonists to tax themselves to support British troops stationed among them; the second imposed import taxes on five basic commodities; the third, passed as a companion piece to the repeal of the Stamp Act, proclaimed that Parliament had the right to legislate for the colonies "in all cases whatsoever." The *Farmer's Letters* were published in twelve installments in a weekly newspaper, the *Pennsylvania Chronicle and Universal Advertiser* (Philadelphia). As installments were issued, other American printers republished them, until they had appeared in all but four of the newspapers in the colonies. They were soon published in pamphlet form in Philadelphia (three editions), Boston (two editions), New York, Williamsburg, Paris, London, and Dublin.

The celebrity that Dickinson won through the *Farmer's Letters* ensured that he would be the principal pensman for the First and Second Continental Congresses in 1774 and 1775 and that he would be among the foremost leaders in those bodies. He wrote most of their petitions to Parliament, to the Crown, and to the British people, including both the conciliatory "Olive Branch Petition" and, with Jefferson as coauthor, the bellicose "Declaration on the Causes and Necessity of Taking up Arms."

Then he came under a cloud. Dickinson wanted to preserve the empire if possible; and if this proved impossible, he thought it imprudent to declare independence until a national government had been created and foreign assistance had been obtained. But by July, 1776, a majority of the delegations in Congress favored declaring independence forthwith. Dickinson could not bring himself to vote for independence, but he and a few others decided to absent themselves when the vote was taken, so Congress could assert that the declaration was unanimous. Despite that, the British regarded Dickinson as responsible for the Revolution, and in December of 1776 their troops, on direct orders, burned his beautiful estate near Philadelphia—a vengeance that Sam and John Adams, John Hancock, the Lees, and Thomas Jefferson were spared.

Dickinson took the sting out of his action by departing immediately for military service. As a colonel of a volunteer battalion, he led the first group of soldiers northward to help defend New York against an expected British invasion. He subsequently resigned his commission, but later, on the occasion of the Battle of Brandywine, he again served on active duty as a private in the Delaware militia. Still later, he returned to Congress, and he served as president of Delaware and then of the Pennsylvania executive council.

Let us pause for a moment to consider a couple of "ifs." If Dickinson had swallowed his scruples and voted for independence, it is probable that he, not Jefferson, would have been chosen to write the Declaration of Independence. We can only speculate as to what a Dickinsonian Declaration would have said, but it seems likely that it would have been based upon English constitutional history rather than, as was Jefferson's, upon natural-rights theory—with vastly different implications. Another "if" concerns the national government. Dickinson drafted the first version of the Articles of Confederation, and his draft, though it reserved to the states control over most internal matters, provided Congress with summary powers in national concerns. An interplay of state and local jealousies resulted in the emasculation of the Articles. If Dickinson's Articles had been adopted, the Constitution might never have been necessary.

But these ifs did not come to pass, and as history marched on, Dickinson had important roles yet to play. He, along with Hamilton and Madison, transformed the Annapolis Convention in 1786 into a call for a general constitutional convention. After the convention, he wrote an influential set of essays supporting ratification of the Constitution that he had so importantly helped to fashion. His last major public service came in 1791/92, when he was one of the main authors of a new constitution for Delaware. Thereafter, though he lived until 1808, he retired from public life. He did follow politics with keen interest, and to the surprise of many contemporaries and most historians, this reluctant rebel and staunch supporter of the Constitution became an ardent Jeffersonian Republican.

THERE SHOULD NOT, HOWEVER, BE ANYTHING SURPRISING about Dickinson's political sentiments during his later years, for if the components of his intellect and temperament are understood, he is to be seen as entirely consistent, start to finish. One seemingly contradictory element is clarified by reference to a rule he made for himself at the outset of his public career. He resolved that he would speak his mind no matter how unpopular his positions might be, but that whenever he was overruled by his countrymen, he would abide by their decision. Hence it was in character for him to have opposed the Declaration of Independence, thereby taking on the wrath of radical patriots, but then to have taken up arms and risked his life for the self-same cause. Precious few, indeed almost none, of those radicals in Congress who spoke most loudly for independence backed their words with deeds.

Somewhat more subtle is the influence of Dickinson's religion upon his politics, for his religious beliefs defy easy categorization. He was a Biblical scholar of considerable depth, and his writings as well as his oratory teemed with quotations from scripture. As indicated, his orientation was toward Quakerism; he said that his real difference with the Friends was that he thought it every man's duty to fight in a just war. On the other hand, he was thoroughly versed in the works of the skeptic David Hume: he could declare, as readily as Hamilton and Madison could, that most men were driven by ambition and avarice and that they must be governed accordingly. Where Dickinson parted company with the likes of Hume, Hamilton, and Madison was in his fundamentally Christian conviction that no matter what governmental institutions one might contrive, a people can be governed successfully only if they are bound together by ties of mutual affection.

More subtle yet is Dickinson's conservatism. All of the major Dickinson scholars—including Charles J. Stillé, J. H. Powell, Trevor Colbourn, David Jacobson, and Milton E. Flower—have agreed that Dickinson was a conservative, in some deep Burkean sense. Perhaps his most quoted line is one he uttered in the Constitutional Convention: "Experience must be our only guide," for "Reason may mislead us." By *experience* he meant not only the events and circumstances that one has personally known but also the entire scope of recorded history. (As he said elsewhere, after making a reference to ancient Greece, "What has been, may be.") In rejecting *reason*, he was spurning the abstract process of thinking deductively from principles to particulars, the mode of reasoning that was fashionable among the philosophes of the French Enlightenment, and he was embracing the empiricism of Sir Francis Bacon, whom he regarded as a truly great thinker.

There is a paradox here, or rather what appears to be a paradox. Colbourn described Dickinson as a "historical revolutionary"; Flower called him a "conservative revolutionary." In ordinary usage these are oxymorons: the adjectives and the noun are mutually exclusive, even if *con-*

servative be defined merely as cautious or prudential. Cautious and prudential men do not make revolutions, nor do men who are guided by the lamp of experience.

The mystery vanishes, however, when we take into account Dickinson's particular understanding of history. His caution and prudence, though doubtless arising in part from natural temperament, were also learned from history and had to do with the timing of actions, not with an unwillingness to act. Tacitus, Dickinson's favorite among the ancient historians, taught him that "misfortune hath happened to many good men, who despising those things which they might *slowly* and *safely* attain, seize them too hastily, and with fatal speed rush upon their own destruction." Repeatedly on the eve of independence, Dickinson pointed to the example of the duke of Monmouth, whose premature rebellion against James II in 1685 had been crushed, whereas William III, "with a *wise delay*, pursued the same views and gloriously mounted a throne" three years later.

Other lessons that Dickinson learned from history were to be found in the Whig interpretation of history, sometimes called the Anglo-Saxon myth. Briefly, that interpretation runs as follows. The Anglo-Saxons, descendants of the noble race described by Tacitus in this *Germania*, long ago had established an agrarian paradise in England. Theirs was a society of landholders, both large and small, who enjoyed security in their liberty and property through the operations of a perfect constitutional system. They had an elective monarch who shared power with elected representatives; justice was dispensed according to the common law by juries and by elective, recallable judges. Men looked after their families and lands, respected one another, and worshipped God freely. When the nation was threatened, they defended it with their militias, to which all men owed service. Their society was untainted by artificial privileges in any form, and priestly castes and standing armies were unknown among them.

Then came the Norman Conquest, achieved not by superior force of arms but by treachery, which taught the lesson that the price of freedom is eternal vigilance. The Normans imposed a system of religion by force and replaced the Saxons' militia and free land tenure with a feudal system of holding land from the king in exchange for military service. The English won back their liberty through Magna Carta in 1215, but from time to time, wicked and designing men oppressed them under new yokes. For more than four and a half centuries, English history was a seesaw struggle between defenders of the ancient constitution and conspirators who sought to impose despotism. The climax came with the seventeenth-century struggle against the Stuart kings and with the triumph of the English people in the Glorious Revolution of 1688/89.

To that point in the story, there was general agreement; as for what happened afterward, there was disagreement. The orthodox English view was that the Glorious Revolution meant the triumph of Parliament—understood to be Crown, Lords, and Commons in one—over would-be royal usurpers. Thenceforth, freedom of religion meant that no Catholic would be king; freedom of the press meant that there would be no prior censorship; freedom of speech meant that no member of Parliament could be prosecuted for anything he said inside Parliament. Otherwise, the liberties of Englishmen were whatever Parliament declared them to be. Said Sir William Blackstone in his *Commentaries on the Laws of England*, a work that Dickinson studied carefully, Parliament was "the place where that absolute despotic power, which must in all governments reside somewhere, is intrusted." Blackstone thought that the rights of Englishmen were adequately protected under such an arrangement.

There was, however, a minority, Oppositionist view in England: that the Glorious Revolution had been betrayed. This view was proclaimed shrilly and repeatedly in newspapers, pamphlets, and books by John Trenchard,

Thomas Gordon, Viscount Bolingbroke, the historian Catharine Macaulay, James Burgh, and others in the "country party" school of thought. The heart of their accusation was that the Whigs, first under the leadership of Sir Robert Walpole (1721–42) and then under every subsequent prime minister, had corrupted the ancient constitution through bribery and distribution of places. The remedy was to restore the constitution by broadening the electorate, abolishing the rotten boroughs, and reinstituting the separation of powers.

Dickinson faced a choice. Which of these conflicting versions was he to believe? He had read the arguments on both sides; in fact Macaulay and Burgh sent him autographed copies of their works out of admiration for his own. And despite the persuasiveness of Blackstone's reasoning, Dickinson clearly opted for the country-party view. Almost certainly the way he leaned was determined by his own observations of English politics. From London in 1754 he had written in horror about the parliamentary elections that were taking place. "There has been above £1,000,000 drawn out of this city already 'for useful purposes at elections, ' " he wrote to his father. "It is astonishing to think what impudence & villainy are practizd on this occasion." He added that voters were required to take an oath that they had not been bribed, but it "is so little regarded that few people can refrain from laughing while they take it." And to his mother he described this open mockery as "one of the greatest proofs perhaps of the corruption of the age."

His propensity to accept the country-party view was reinforced by his knowledge of ancient history. He had read most deeply in Roman history of the first century B.C., a time when the republic was wracked and eventually destroyed by a succession of conspiracies. There is evidence that he saw himself as an American Cicero (which incidentally is what Voltaire called him), and it is to be recalled that the climax of Cicero's career had been the unmasking of Catiline's conspiracy. Knowing what he knew of Rome, it was easy enough for Dickinson to believe that evil men had corrupted the English constitution and, from 1765 onward, had designed to destroy American liberty.

That is the key to the seeming paradox of Dickinson as a historical or conservative revolutionary. In his own eyes he was no kind of revolutionary at all; he was, rather, a historical conservative. From 1765 to 1776 he saw himself as laboring to preserve the empire and restore the ancient constitution. When his efforts failed, he addressed himself to the preservation of traditional American liberties through the instrumentality of the states and to the preservation of the Union through the creation of a substitute for the old and hallowed order.

That is what he went to Philadelphia to accomplish in May of 1787.

AS ONE FOLLOWS DICKINSON THROUGH THE CONVEN-tion there are a few immediate particulars to bear in mind. He had never been physically strong; he was frail almost to the point of emaciation; and he was ill throughout that summer. No doubt this explains why William Pierce, the member from Georgia who recorded his impressions of the delegates, was disappointed in Dickinson as an orator and why Dickinson did not deliver any extremely long speeches. Another point is that his personal experience in politics had taught him to be wary of excessive democracy: Delaware politics could be violent and vicious, and the political arena in Pennsylvania was, in the words of Benjamin Rush, a "dung cart."

Furthermore, in the convention Dickinson represented Delaware, which had specific, tangible interests, most notably a desire to obtain a share in the vast domain of western lands claimed by several states and the Congress. But Dickinson had long since worked out principles to guide him when acting in a representative capacity. At base he followed his conscience and his best judgment of the public interest. Then, if the interests of his state conflicted with those of another state, he put his state first. If, however, his state's interests conflicted with those of the nation, the nation took precedence.

Thus guided by principle, prepared by learning and experience, and motivated by the mission of conserving and restoring that had inspired him for more than two decades, John Dickinson took his seat in the convention on Tuesday, May 29, 1787.

On that day, Edmund Randolph "opened the main business" by introducing the fifteen resolutions known as the Virginia Plan. Though Dickinson thought much of the Virginia Plan acceptable, he found some features totally objectionable. He agreed that the national government should be reorganized by establishing executive and judicial branches and a bicameral legislature. He agreed that the legislature should be given a general grant of power "to legislate in all cases to which the separate States are incompetent, or in which the harmony of the United States may be interrupted by the exercise of individual Legislation," for that is what he had proposed in his original draft of the Articles of Confederation. But he found intolerable the proposal to empower the national government to use force against any state "failing to fulfill its duty." He also objected to the proposal that the executive and judicial branches should constitute a "council of revision" with power to veto acts of the national legislature; this he regarded as an improper violation of the principle of the separation of powers. And most vehemently, he was against the proposal to abandon the existing system, wherein each state had one vote, in favor of a system in which representation in both houses would be apportioned on the basis of population or wealth.

Nor did Dickinson find acceptable the alternative "small states plan," which William Paterson of New Jersey proposed on June 15. The Paterson Plan would have granted

Congress extensive enumerated powers and would have added executive and judicial branches, but Congress would have remained a unicameral body in which each state had one vote. When it was introduced, Dickinson said to Madison, "you see the consequences of pushing things too far." Madison and his allies had mistakenly assumed that every delegate who held out for equal representation in one branch of Congress was opposed to a national government. Dickinson tried to explain to him that many such delegates were "friends to a good National Government" but would "sooner submit to a foreign power" than be totally deprived of equal suffrage "and thereby be thrown under the domination of the large states."

Dickinson himself had made his position clear. It was a wise one, and it was to prevail: he wanted the national legislature to be modeled as closely as possible upon the British Parliament, in which one house represented the "common" people and was periodically elected and the other represented the hereditary baronies in perpetuity. As it happened, most of the delegates admired the British constitution but could see no way by which Americans could adapt it to their use. During the first week of debates, Dickinson offered a profoundly helpful insight. Because of what he called the "accidental lucky division of this country into states," America had a structural substitute for the English baronies: the states were, in a sense, both hereditary and permanent. It was, therefore, prudence and wisdom to draw one branch of the national legislature immediately from the people, as in the House of Commons, and to have the other branch represent the states and be chosen by the state legislatures, "through such a refining process as will assimilate it as near as may be to the House of Lords." Such a mixed system, he added, "was as politic as it was unavoidable."

It is commonly asserted that the scheme of representation in Congress—proportional to population in the House and equally by states in the Senate—came about as the result of the "Connecticut compromise." In fact, it was not a compromise, and it did not originate with the Connecticut delegation. Rather, it was the position advocated by Dickinson at the outset, one that gained adherents as other delegates came to appreciate the astuteness of his analysis.

Dickinson shortly won a major though incomplete victory. On June 7 he moved that the members of the Senate be elected by the state legislatures. The motion implied, but only implied, an equality of representation in the Senate, for it was generally understood that the Senate was to be much smaller than the House. Accordingly, the most ardent advocates of proportional representation in both houses—Madison, James Wilson, Gouverneur Morris, and Charles Pinckney—argued strongly against the proposal. Dickinson carried the point. His motion for election by the state legislatures was approved, eleven states to none, but that still left the basis of representation in the Senate undecided.

Indeed, it was the unwillingness of the large states to concede equality in the Senate that led delegates from the small states to formulate the Paterson Plan. The Paterson and Randolph plans were discussed and compared on Friday June 15 and again on Saturday. It was clear to Dickinson that neither plan would work and that neither side was willing to compromise. He therefore spent the rest of the weekend fashioning a set of resolutions that combined the best of both plans with some ideas of his own. Dickinson's proposals were closer to the finished constitution than was either of the two plans, and had his resolutions been adopted, they would have saved more than a month of debate.

But fate intervened: Alexander Hamilton had the same idea. On Monday June 18, Dickinson offered the first of his resolutions. But before it could be discussed, Hamilton, who had hitherto been reticent, took the floor to deliver a speech that consumed the whole day's session: he concluded it by presenting a high-toned constitution of his own. In the circumstances, and after his first resolution was rejected the next day, Dickinson decided that it would be best to wait for a more seasonable opportunity.

During the next two weeks the delegates remained deadlocked, and as the heat of the summer grew daily more oppressive, tempers rose. On June 30 Gunning Bedford, another delegate from Delaware, alarmed the convention by declaring that if the large states stubbornly refused to accommodate the needs of the small states, "the small states will find some foreign ally of more honor and good faith, who will take them by the hand and do them justice." That same day Dickinson was working feverishly on the notes for a speech urging compromise and moderation. The notes, which have come to light only in recent years, are full; from them it is clear that had he delivered the speech, it would have been one of the longest, most impassioned, and most eloquent of his career.

But he did not deliver it. Exhausted by his efforts, debilitated by the heat, and severely ill, he found it necessary to go home for rest and quiet. He seems to have returned briefly on July 9 or 10; on those days the convention debated a proposal to count slaves for purposes of representation (which he staunchly opposed), and notes of the debates in Dickinson's hand have survived. But if so, he soon left again; the next time he is recorded as speaking was on July 25, and his remarks suggest an extended absence. Thus he was not present when Franklin proposed the real compromise, that the House of Representatives have exclusive power to originate money bills, in exchange for which representation in the Senate would be equal; and he was not present when the delegates from the Carolinas and Connecticut, who had supported his dual conception of the basis of representation, worked out the backstage deals that led to the approval of the compromise. But if the political achievement belonged to others, the idea nonetheless was Dickinson's.

He was less influential in determining the make-up of the executive branch—except in a negative sense—for he was mistrustful of executive power. He wrote that he could find in history "no instance" in which the executive authority in a republic had been lodged "with safety" in a single person; accordingly, he was one of the dozen or so delegates who favored a plural executive. When a single executive was decided upon, he proposed that the president be removable upon application of a majority of the state legislatures. He opposed the election of the president by Congress, which remained part of the scheme of things until early September. At that time he was serving on a committee charged with taking care of unfinished parts of the constitution, and according to his later recollection (which may not be entirely accurate), he made a short, ardent speech before that committee which inspired its members to propose an alternative way of electing the president: the electoral-college system. Once that system had been adopted he no longer feared that the executive branch would jeopardize American liberty.

Dickinson was less optimistic about the judicial branch. He was convinced that a national court system needed to be established, but he was fearful of judicial usurpation. When it was suggested that the Supreme Court, as an inherent part of its duties, would have the power to declare acts of Congress unconstitutional, he was appalled. Citing the medieval example of the kingdom of Aragon in Spain, he suggested prophetically that when judges began "to set aside the law," they tended to expand their decrees until they transformed themselves into legislators. So fearful was he of judicial self-aggrandizement that he proposed that judges be removable by the president on application by both houses of Congress.

Dickinson failed to have his way in another matter of importance to him. He firmly opposed slavery, and he had freed the slaves that he had inherited from his father. In the convention, he sought to prevent the constitution from encouraging slavery in any way. Though he recognized that the institution of slavery was a matter of state, not national, concern, he argued that the importation of slaves was a "question which ought to be left to the National Govt. not to the States." He had held that upon the adoption of the Declaration of Independence, slaves *"could not afterwards be imported into these states,"* and in the convention he declared it "inadmissible on every principle of honor & safety that the importation of slaves should be authorized to the States by the Constitution." When the convention voted to exempt the slave trade from congressional regulation for twenty years, it avoided the word *slave* and referred instead to "the migration or importation of such persons as the several States now existing shall think proper to admit." Dickinson thought this was rank hypocrisy, and he moved that the phrase· "the slave trade" should be substituted instead. "The omitting of this *word,*" he said, "will be regarded as an Endeavor to conceal a principle of which we are ashamed." His motion was unanimously rejected.

DICKINSON'S CONTRIBUTION TO THE CAMPAIGN FOR ratification was his *Letters of Fabius*, published in April of 1788. To appreciate the significance of his effort, we must consider the immediate political context. Five states had ratified quickly: Delaware first, Pennsylvania and New Jersey before the end of 1787, Georgia and Connecticut early in January of 1788. Then the momentum was broken. Massachusetts approved by a narrow margin early in February, but New Hampshire's convention adjourned without reaching a decision, though it resolved to reconvene in June. Meanwhile, after a feeble start, anti-Federalists began to be better organized and to grind out large quantities of propaganda against the Constitution. Alarmed by this development, Dickinson took up his pen.

Read two hundred years later, the *Letters of Fabius* do not have the power, the coherence, or the breadth of the *Federalist* essays; but in 1788 they may well have been as persuasive because of the nature of Dickinson's rhetorical strategy. As a student of the classical rhetorical arts, he was aware that the first premise of an argument must rest on the "reputable beliefs of the audience." The reputable beliefs to which anti-Federalists appealed, through their choice of phraseology, were those of the English country party Oppositionists and the American Patriots of the sixties and seventies. Dickinson was a past master of that idiom, and he turned it effectively against his anti-Federalist adversaries. He was also aware of the importance of zeal. In the *Farmer's Letters* he had analyzed what it was that made the rhetoric of Lord Camden and William Pitt so powerful: "Their reasoning is not only just—it is . . . 'vehement.' " In the *Letters of Fabius*, Dickinson himself was vehement, freely using, in addition to his trademark Biblical exhortations and classical citations, such emotionally ladened catchwords as *licentiousness, vice, luxury, corruption,* and *tyranny* and such scornful phrases as "foreign fashions" and "rebellion against heaven."

But rhetorical strategy is one thing; the message is another. Characteristically, Dickinson justified the Constitution in terms of history and prudence, almost as if he were defending the ancient constitution of England. Indeed, astute readers would have noticed that he often employed well-known passages that had originally been used to praise that constitution. He paraphrased Blackstone, for instance, when he said that the Constitution united "force, wisdom, and benevolence," and he paraphrased Burke when he wrote of "animated moderation" and when he described the Constitution as "ever new, and always the same." Dickinson did so because he wanted his readers to understand what he understood—namely, that the American Constitution was the product of history, not of theory. He reinforced that message, and incidentally made a summing-up personal statement, by identifying himself as Fabius, after the Roman general who had saved the republic through caution, prudence, patience, and persistence.

That is our penultimate comment. The last is this: John Dickinson was a man whose services to his country should ensure his enduring fame. Perhaps we can best enshrine his memory by taking seriously the concluding words of his second letter of Fabius. The Constitution, he pointed out, is written "in the most clear, strong, positive, unequivocal expressions, of which our language is capable. Magna charta, or any other law, never contained clauses more decisive and emphatic. While the people of these states have sense, they will understand them; and while they have spirit, they will make them to be observed."

6

NE PHILOSOPHIS
AUDIAMUS: THE MIDDLE
DELEGATES IN THE
CONSTITUTIONAL
CONVENTION

HISTORIANS OF THE CONSTITUTIONAL CONVENTION
have agreed that there were divisions among the delegates, but they have disagreed as to what those divisions
were and what underlay them. It was long believed that
the only significant line of division was between small
states and large ones. Delegates from the small states, according to this view, were less nationalistic and less far-
sighted than those from the large states: they thought the
"exigencies of the Union" could be met simply by vesting
a few additional powers in the unicameral Congress of
the Articles of Confederation, in which each state had one
vote. Delegates from the large states, by contrast, saw the
need for an overhaul of the existing system so as to establish separate legislative, executive, and judicial branches;
to divide the legislative branch into two houses, representation in both of which should be made proportional to
the population of the states; and to vest the national government with coercive power in all matters of national concern. The intransigence of the small states made necessary
the famous "Connecticut Compromise," whereby the
states were given equal representation in one house and
representation proportional to population in the other;
but otherwise the large-states nationalists, led by

James Madison, James Wilson, and Gouverneur Morris, had their way.

Variations of that scenario still prevail in textbook accounts and in the official line hewed by the Bicentennial Commission, even though scholars have long since demonstrated its lack of resemblance to what happened in Philadelphia during the summer of 1787. For openers, the split over representation was not one between the more-populous and the less-populous states. If the extremes (Virginia, the mammoth, and Delaware, the midget) are omitted, the average population of the states voting for equal representation was roughly 278,000 and that of the states favoring proportional representation was about 307,000, a difference of only 10 percent. The alignment on the question was primarily sectional: all four states south of the Potomac voted in one camp, and those to the north voted six to two in the other. Secondarily, it reflected the division between states that had claims to western lands and those that did not. Moreover, the compromise did not originate with the Connecticut delegates. The first to propose it was William Pierce of Georgia on May 31; the second was John Dickinson of Delaware on June 2. The traditional view also leaves out of account the realignments that took place after the compromise was adopted on July 16. Finally, the delegates in the early "large-states" bloc proved not to be appreciably more nationalistic than those in the opposite bloc, and Madison, Wilson, and Morris were frustrated on many issues that they themselves considered significant.

The alignments in the convention—notice the plural—can be and have been fruitfully studied by analyzing the shifting patterns of voting behavior as the convention unfolded. Probably the most sophisticated such study is that published in 1981 by Calvin C. Jillson, who found that coalitions realigned themselves during each of four phases of the convention. The traditional "small" vs. "large" alignment prevailed until the adoption of the compromise on representation. A different coalition, which pitted the two northernmost and the three southernmost states against the six states in between, then arose and held until August 28. The discussion of certain issues concerning states' rights and states' powers brought about a short-lived (August 29 to September 3) return to a large-versus-small alignment. From September 4 to the end of the convention on September 17, Pennsylvania, Virginia, and the Carolinas formed one bloc, in opposition to the seven other states that were present.

Despite its significant contributions, however, Jillson's analysis is marked by certain weaknesses. Some are inherent in any quantitative study of voting patterns—the tendency to think of numbers as being reality, rather than as the abstract symbols that they are; the ignoring of motivation, tactics, and qualitative differences among issues; and other subtle considerations. Another difficulty is that certain blocs remained constant throughout the four phases: Pennsylvania and Virginia; the two Carolinas; and Connecticut, Maryland, and New Jersey. Moreover, Delaware stayed with the last of these blocs except during the six days of the third phase; and New Hampshire, whose delegation arrived only after the end of the first phase, sided with Massachusetts to the end. Finally, the study of voting patterns tells us nothing about the attitudes and behavior of the individual delegates, since votes were cast by states.

A better understanding of the alignments in the convention can be reached by approaching the delegates as human beings rather than as representatives of ideological positions or interest groups. We have, after all, fairly abundant (though far from complete) records of the debates, and the private correspondence and political writings of many of the delegates are available. From these sources it is possible to obtain a firm grip on the beliefs, attitudes, prejudices, and values of the principal characters among the Framers. It is also possible to gain a feeling for such intangible qualities as temperament, personality, and ability—qualities that are not susceptible to measurement but arguably are of critical importance in determining whether the convention would succeed.

Let us illustrate by reference to Alexander Hamilton and Elbridge Gerry, both of whom went into the convention convinced that it was necessary to strengthen and reorganize the national authority. Hamilton was a man of towering genius, a flexible and creative imagination, and superb gifts as a speaker; but in the words of William Pierce, "his manners are tinctured with stiffness, and sometimes with a degree of vanity that is highly disagreeable." Gerry, by contrast, was a plodding sort, well educated but dull, a republican ideologue and a protégé of Samuel Adams who had been jarred loose from his jealousy of national power by the trauma of Shays' Rebellion; he was also a "hesitating and laborious speaker" who got on people's nerves and was himself extremely thin-skinned. It was almost inevitable that if Hamilton and Gerry were to occupy the same room for any considerable length of time, they would clash resoundingly. And it was as likely that Hamilton would have supported any constitution produced by the convention as it was that Gerry would have disapproved it. A wide assortment of similar comparisons could be made.

On such personal bases, it is possible to group the delegates into three general camps. The first would include those who were thoroughly convinced that the national authority must be strengthened, though of course within limits. The group would have two subdivisions: ideologues, whose attitudes were grounded in abstract philosophy and political theory (Madison, Wilson, and Charles Pinckney, for example), and nonideologues, whose attitudes were grounded in experience (Robert Morris, Gouverneur Morris, and Washington, for example). The second group would include those who had serious reservations about altering the balance of power between states and nation. This group also had two subdivisions: country-party ideologues, who were willing to strengthen the national authority only if its powers seemed to them to be distributed in accordance with theoretical doctrines laid down by the likes of Trenchard and Gordon, Bolingbroke, and Montesquieu (George Mason, Edmund Randolph, and William Livingston, for example), and state particularists, who were scarcely willing to strengthen the national authority at all (John Lansing, Jr., Robert Yates, and Luther Martin, for example).

The third group comprised those who might be described as the "middle delegates," who took a stance that was partly national, partly federal. The major figures in this group were Roger Sherman, Oliver Ellsworth, and William Samuel Johnson of Connecticut; John Dickinson of Delaware; John Rutledge, Charles Cotesworth Pinckney, and Pierce Butler of South Carolina; and Hugh Williamson of North Carolina. These men did not see eye to eye on every issue, and on some matters they were strongly opposed to one another. What they shared were wisdom, a Burkean kind of conservatism, practicality, and a belief in Dickinson's maxim that "Experience must be our only guide," for "Reason may mislead us." Or in the words of Petronius, *"Ne philosophis audiamus"*: Let us not listen to philosophers.

IT MAY BE USEFUL TO INTRODUCE THE "MIDDLE DELE-gates," since most are not at all well known even to scholars who specialize in the period. Proceeding in alphabetical order permits us to begin with the most obscure, Pierce Butler. Butler was born into a noble Anglo-Irish family, that of the dukes of Ormandy, which bought him a commission in the British army when he was eleven years old. He began active service at the age of fourteen, and he was among the troops sent to Boston in 1770. The next year he married a daughter of one of the wealthiest

South Carolina plantation families and moved to his wife's native colony. Subsequently he resigned his commission as a major. Little is known of his education, though it seems that he was steeped in the classics (he sent his son to be educated in a classical school in Chelsea, England, wishing to make the son "a replica of himself"). A superficial reading of the records of the convention would make it seem that he had little on his mind beyond protecting the institution of slavery. More careful scrutiny makes it possible to place him with fair precision in the eighteenth-century political spectrum. His endorsement of landed-property qualifications for voting and officeholding (see Madison's *Notes*, August 7 and elsewhere), his vehement speech regarding corruption and patronage under George II and his warm approval of "the great Montesquieu" (see Yates's *Secret Proceedings*, June 23), his diatribe against "the Blood-suckers who had speculated on the distresses of others" by buying depreciated public securities (see Madison, August 23), and his reference to "the Constitution of Britain, *when in its purity,*" as a model (see letter to Weedon Butler, October 8, italics added)—all these establish him as a firm, though by no means rigidly ideological, adherent of the English country-party values associated with Viscount Bolingbroke and his Tory circle.

John Dickinson's views and career were considered in the preceding chapter.

Oliver Ellsworth, who was born in Connecticut in 1745, was educated at Princeton and subsequently studied theology and law. He struggled as a lawyer at first, but he had built up a solid practice and a considerable state-wide reputation by the time he first served in the Continental Congress in 1778, and in 1787 he was a judge on the Connecticut Superior Court. Though he was a man of learning, he disdained all affectation and ornament: both his speeches and his political writings were marked by a blunt, hard-nosed, common-sense style. Nor was there a trace of abstract ideology or speculative theory in his make-up. He knew what he wanted for himself, for his state, and for his country, and he knew how to go about getting it. What is most important to understand about Ellsworth is that he was a shrewd bargainer and a tough, skillful, and when he found it necessary, unscrupulous political operator.

If Ellsworth was self-consciously a self-made man, his colleague William Samuel Johnson was born to a station of quality. He was among the best educated of all the delegates, having degrees from Yale and Harvard and having a considerable reputation as a classical scholar; he was to serve as president of Columbia College from 1787 to 1800. He had been Connecticut's agent in London from 1766 to 1771, and his standing in the state was so high that although he was a Loyalist sympathizer if not actually a Tory during the war, he was unharmed despite the violence with which his fellow citizens treated most Tories. As soon as the war was over, he was made a member of Congress for his state. He was one with Ellsworth and Sherman in regard to all major subjects that arose before the convention, and he lent the delegation a great deal of prestige and dignity. At almost sixty, he was the second-oldest of the middle delegates.

Charles Cotesworth Pinckney, at forty-one, was the junior member of the group, but he was far from junior in his qualifications. As a child he had been in England with his parents and his younger brother Thomas (later celebrated for the Pinckney Treaty with Spain) when his father suddenly died. His mother returned to South Carolina but left her two boys to be educated in England. They received rigorous training in classical studies before entering and earning degrees at Oxford and then returning home. At Oxford, Charles Cotesworth heard the lectures that were subsequently published as Sir William Blackstone's *Commentaries on the Laws of England*. The Pinckney brothers' Anglicization reduced their American patriotism not at all, and when they came back to South Carolina, they embraced the American cause ardently. Charles Cotesworth, who had undertaken advanced study in chemistry, botany, and military science in France, became a captain in the South Carolina line in 1775. He served on active duty until the end of the war, retiring as a brigadier general. Like the other delegates from his state, he favored a strengthened national authority but regarded the protection of the slave trade and exemption of exports from taxation as *sine qua non*.

Heading the South Carolina delegation, by virtue of seniority—he was forty-eight—as well as experience, ability, and force of personality, was John Rutledge. Like Dickinson and C. C. Pinckney, Rutledge had studied law at the Middle Temple. He was the leading member of a high-ranking family in the rice-plantation aristocracy, owning plantations that employed more than two hundred slaves. He had also netted £9,000 sterling annually from his law practice before the Revolution. Neither status nor wealth inhibited him from embracing the American revolutionary cause: like Dickinson, he was a member of the Stamp Act Congress in 1765, and he attended the First and the Second Continental Congress. So patriotic that he named one of his sons States, he nonetheless managed to tend to the interests of South Carolina, seeing to it, for example, that rice exports were exempted from the various trade boycotts adopted by Congress. The same attention to both national interests and those of his state governed his conduct in the convention. He was an accomplished orator, even though, perhaps because of the quickness of his mind, he often spoke too rapidly. He was a shrewd, realistic bargainer (a man of "Design and Cunning," John Adams called him), which made it easy for him to collaborate with Sherman and Ellsworth despite their differences in background.

Sherman was a truly professional politician. Self-made and self-taught, he had been a shoemaker and surveyor in his youth, had held at least one public office, and usually two or three, for forty-two consecutive years, and had been a judge of the Connecticut Superior Court for twenty-one years. William Pierce's sketch of him is penetrating. "Mr. Sherman," Pierce wrote, "exhibits the oddest shaped character I ever remember to have met with. He is awkward, un-meaning, and unaccountably strange in his manner." His thinking was deep and comprehensive, but "the oddity of his address, the vulgarisms that accompany his public speaking, and that strange New England cant" in which he spoke made "everything that is connected with him grotesque and laughable." Yet, Pierce added, "no Man has a better Heart or a clearer Head." Most tellingly, "He is an able politician, and extremely artful in accomplishing any particular object;—it is remarked that he seldom fails." Pierce did not say so, but Sherman's "particular object" was clear to everyone who had seen him operate in Congress. Connecticut was greatly overpopulated, given the quality of its land and the state of agricultural technology, and Sherman was seeking for his state a claim to lands elsewhere, either in north-central Pennsylvania or in Congress' Northwest Territory.

Hugh Williamson was a man of such broad experience and such diversified learning that he may almost be regarded as a younger (he was fifty-one) Benjamin Franklin. He took a B.A. at the College of Philadelphia in 1757, became a Presbyterian clergyman, and took an M.A. in 1760, after which he was a professor of mathematics. Then he went abroad to study science and medicine at Edinburgh and Utrecht, whence he returned after eight years to settle in North Carolina and practice medicine. During the war he was surgeon general in the North Carolina line; afterward he served in Congress. Like the other middle delegates, he would support stronger national government, provided that something special in the arrangements would favor his state. He was amenable to any such that might arise, and his prestige among his fellows from North

Carolina put him in a good bargaining position because he could "deliver" his state's vote on almost any issue.

Several general remarks can be made about these delegates. They were older and more mature than most of the other delegates (their average age was fifty-one and their mean age was fifty, as compared, for example, with an average of thirty-nine and a mean of thirty-five for the seven most outspoken nationalists in the convention: Madison, Gouverneur Morris, Charles Pinckney, Wilson, Nathaniel Gorham, Hamilton, and Rufus King). They were experienced in public affairs, having served a combined total of 165 years in a wide range of public offices—military, legislative, executive, and judicial. With the exceptions of Ellsworth and Sherman, they were cosmopolitan, all the others having spent several years abroad. Except for Sherman, all had received extensive formal education and were men of great learning. All had particular axes to grind, different but compatible; none was bound by ideological fetters; and all were highly skilled in the political arts. If they could get together—and they did—these eight would form a multitude.

DURING THE OPENING DAYS OF THE CONVENTION THE middle delegates were in opposite camps. On May 30, the first day after Randolph had introduced his resolutions calling for an enlarged and reorganized national authority, the Connecticut and Delaware delegates insisted on preserving the existing Confederation, whereas—despite C. C. Pinckney's expressed doubts as to the legality of departing from the Articles—both Carolina delegations supported the Virginia Plan. Moreover, the Carolinians favored proportional representation in both houses of Congress throughout the early debate on that subject, and the Connecticut men and Dickinson, along with the rest of the Delaware delegation, were for equal representation in at least one house.

But the possibility that there were grounds for accommodation soon became evident. Almost at the beginning, advocates of equal representation recognized that they could not have their way in regard to both houses, and they conceded the lower house and directed their efforts toward equality in the Senate. It was in this context that Dickinson gave his pair of speeches (June 2 and 6) that provided a conceptual breakthrough by likening the states to baronies and proposing that the Senate be thought of as an American version of the House of Lords. As indicated, the lower house would be "drawn immediately from the people," and the upper would be elected by the state legislatures. It quickly came to light that the aristocratic South Carolinians, distrusting all popular elections and having effectively closed the rabble out of their own legislature, wanted both houses of Congress to be chosen by and dependent on the state legislatures. When Wilson and Madison attacked Dickinson's proposal by pointing out that it implied at least relative equality in the Senate, since that branch was to have few members, others from the "small states" (including Sherman and Ellsworth, who at first were opposed to it) reversed positions and promptly endorsed the idea. Dickinson's depiction of the states as substitutes for baronies appealed to many in the large-states bloc as well, and thus, though the convention had rejected such a motion on May 31, it now approved Dickinson's proposal by a unanimous vote of the delegations present.

During the next week, two more ingredients of a possible deal became evident. One was that the South Carolinians wanted representation in Congress to be based, not on numbers of people, but on the wealth of the individual states, or on a combination of numbers and wealth. The other was that George Read, Dickinson's Delaware colleague, let it be known that his insistence upon equal representation arose from a desire to obtain for his state a share in the "common lands" that "the great states have appropriated to themselves" (see Madison, June 11, and Yates, June 25). Delegates from New Jersey and Maryland would reveal the same motivation, indicating that they shared the same tangible goal as Connecticut.

Exactly who agreed privately with whom to do what and when cannot be known for certain: backstage maneuvers are, by their nature, secret and are normally undocumented: but from the recorded proceedings of the convention the identity of the participants and the general outlines of their agreements can be unmistakably inferred. The Connecticut delegates supported the South Carolinians in regard to slavery, exports, and—after a fashion—basing representation on wealth, although they had no direct interest in doing so. The South Carolinians, in turn, supported Connecticut in regard to lands and, indirectly, through the agency of Williamson and the North Carolina delegation, equal representation in the Senate, even though it was not in the direct interest of either of the Carolinas to do so. What North Carolina received from the trading will become evident below.

The first portent that machinations were in the offing came on June 11, when Rutledge and Butler suggested that representation be based upon the quotas of direct taxation levied by Congress against the several states; the quotas themselves were based upon the estimated value of lands. Dickinson countered that representation should be based upon sums actually contributed, not upon assessments, which would make it in the interest of the states to pay their quotas. Rufus King effectively closed those approaches by pointing out that the future federal revenues would be derived largely from import duties, which might preclude the "non-importing" states (Connecticut, Delaware, and New Jersey) from having any representatives at all.

Resolution of the question regarding the basis of representation began three weeks later. After a tie vote indicated that the convention was hopelessly deadlocked, a committee of all the states was chosen to try to find an acceptable compromise (July 2). On July 5 the committee reported its proposal that representation in the Senate be equal by states but that all money bills must originate in the "popular branch" and could not be amended by the Senate. During the next few days, while "large states" delegates grumbled that the money power was of no consequence, the South Carolinians insisted that representation in the House be based at least partly on wealth (July 5 and 9). Then, on July 11, Williamson proposed that representation be based upon the number of free inhabitants and three-fifths of the number of slaves, which from a southern point of view did in fact combine numbers and wealth. The South Carolinians held out for fully counting slaves— almost certainly as a ploy, designed to make counting three-fifths of the slaves seem like a compromise to the many northerners who opposed counting them at all. Williamson's motion was rejected, but the next day, after it was decided to interconnect direct taxes and representation, Ellsworth moved the three-fifths clause again, and over some northern opposition, the motion passed.

That, as the North Carolina delegates wrote their governor the day after the convention adjourned, was a bonanza for their state. It meant not only that slaves would not be taxed fully, even if Congress should resort to head taxes, but also that taxes on land would be the same in southern states as in the "Eastern States," even though "we certainly have, one with another, land of twice the value that they Possess." In sum, North Carolina and the other southern states would obtain more than a fair share of representatives and would carry less than a fair share of the burden of taxes.

Now it was time for Williamson to repay Connecticut for the favor, and he did so. On July 16 the final vote on equal representation in the Senate was taken, and North Carolina abandoned the "large states" camp. Its vote, when coupled with Massachusetts' divided vote, tipped the outcome in favor of equality. What Ellsworth was the first to call a "partly national, partly federal" system—which all the middle delegates approved in principle and all the nationalists opposed in principle—would become a reality.

Some mysteries about the private trading remain. Williamson later claimed (August 9) that North Carolina "had agreed to an equality in the Senate merely in consideration that money bills should be confined to the other House"; but that claim is in direct contradiction to his statement on July 5 that the compromise proposal was "the most objectionable of any he had yet heard" and his comment on July 7 that if power over money bills were to be limited, it should be confined to the Senate, not to the House. It is almost certain that he was being less than candid in August; and in light of the support that Connecticut had given to North Carolina regarding the three-fifths clause and also in light of the close cooperation among Ellsworth, Sherman, Rutledge, and Williamson that would be manifest in August, it likewise appears that a three-way deal regarding representation had been worked out late in June or early in July.

What Connecticut got out of the arrangement, apart from equal representation, was special protection for its claims to western land. It already had a claim to the Western Reserve in the Ohio country and a tenuous claim to the Susquehannah lands in Pennsylvania; but the former, conceded by the Confederation Congress, could be taken away if equality of representation were abolished, and the latter had no prospect of being successfully prosecuted since it could be adjudicated only in the courts of Pennsylvania. To protect Connecticut's interests, Rutledge and Ellsworth, as members of the five-man Committee of Detail (July 26–August 4), saw to it that article II of the committee's draft entrusted to the supervision of the Senate all territorial and jurisdictional disputes between states. Had that provision stood, equality of votes in the Senate would have protected Connecticut's claim to the Western

Reserve, for the landless states were in a majority and had a common interest in supporting one another's claims.

But the question became more complex during the recess. Sherman went home to New Haven to attend the funeral of a friend, and as he was passing through New York, he learned of the consummation of an agreement between Congress and the Ohio Company (a Connecticut-dominated company in which other New Englanders had also invested), whereby the company acquired a million acres of western land. That made it seem that Connecticut's ability to protect its interest in the Senate would now be less than in the federal courts, where the subject would be removed from politics altogether. This idea was reinforced on August 25, when the convention adopted a proposed clause that "all debts contracted & engagements entered into, by or under the authority of Congs. shall be as valid agst the U. States under this constitution as under the Confederation." The resolution was designed to apply to public debts, but the words "& engagements entered into" would make it apply to the Western Reserve and the Ohio Company purchase as well. Accordingly, on August 24, Rutledge and Sherman arranged that the settlement of land claims be transferred from the Senate to the federal courts.

MEMBERS OF THE MIDDLE BLOC OF DELEGATES HAD A decisive influence upon the make-up of the executive branch as well as the legislative, but in this matter their contributions derived from creativity and intelligence, rather than from connivance and intrigue. They shared a common attitude toward executive power—namely, a distrust of it, tempered by a recognition that it was necessary. At first they, like the rest of the delegates, could not agree on a means of constituting an executive branch that would be both adequately energetic and not dangerous. To that end, Sherman, Dickinson, and Williamson favored a plural executive, as being safest; the others thought a plural executive would be neither energetic nor responsible. Connecticut and South Carolina supported a motion to make the executive removable by Congress, which would have opened the way for a ministerial system, and Delaware supported Dickinson's motion that Congress be empowered to remove the executive on the application of a majority of the state legislatures (June 2).

The make-up of the executive branch was debated vigorously between the adoption of the compromise regarding representation and the recess on July 26. The general sense of the convention was that Congress should elect the executive, but all delegates recognized flaws in such a scheme of things. Elections would be vulnerable to intrigue and corruption, especially by foreign powers; and everyone remembered how such intrigue had led to the dismemberment of Poland. Moreover, if the executive were eligible for reelection, he would be dependent upon Congress, and if he were not, he would have to be elected for a dangerously long term. Exploring the alternative of a decentralized election, either by popular vote or by electors, the delegates encountered what appeared to be an insuperable obstacle: because of habitual loyalties and the difficulty of communication, the electors would be likely to vote for someone from their own states, no candidate would receive a majority, and the choice would fall upon Congress. Williamson offered a way around that barrier by suggesting that electors should vote for three candidates, in which case they probably would cast only one vote for a person from their own state. Gouverneur Morris immediately seized the idea and improved upon it, proposing that the electors vote for two persons, "one of whom at least should not be of his own State." But Gerry and Mason, suddenly frightened by the prospect that any decentralized election might be dominated by an aristocratic junto "of men dispersed through the Union & acting in Concert"—the Society of the Cincinnati, for example—

objected strongly (July 25). Moreover, delegates from the extreme northern and southern states, assuming that electors, however chosen, would meet in one place to vote, protested that their states would thereby be effectively disfranchised (July 26). Thus the idea of a decentralized election was dropped, and the convention voted once again that the executive be chosen by Congress for a seven-year term and not be eligible for reelection.

That was the way matters stood when the Committee of Detail began its labors, and because no one on the committee trusted an executive thus elected, the members were loath to vest the branch with substantive power. Accordingly, in their draft they proposed that most of the traditional executive power be vested in Congress, except that the power to appoint judges and ambassadors and the treaty-making power would be lodged exclusively in the Senate (articles 7, 9, 10). That would have made the presidency little more than a titular office.

It was Pierce Butler who devised the solution. Butler was a member of a committee composed of one delegate from each state, appointed on August 31 to resolve a number of unsettled questions. He proposed a method of electing the president that overcame all the objections to other methods. His proposal provided for a president and a vice-president, which satisfied those who had been concerned about the succession in the event of the death or the disability of the president. It provided that electors be chosen as the individual state legislatures should determine, which assuaged those who feared popular election by permitting the legislatures themselves to choose the electors. Each state was to be allotted a number of electors equal to its combined seats in both houses of Congress, which reflected the earlier compromise on representation. The plan provided that electors would meet in their own states, which obviated the problem of distance and minimized the probability of intrigue. Since a president so chosen would be sufficiently independent of Congress, he could be safely entrusted—this was part of the proposal—with power to appoint ambassadors, judges, and other officers, with the concurrence of the Senate, and with the power to make treaties, with the consent of two-thirds of the Senate (September 4; see Butler to Weedon Butler, May 5, 1788).

Only one significant change was made in Butler's scheme, and it was proposed by Williamson and Sherman. The Butler plan provided that if no candidate received a majority of the electoral votes—which most assumed would normally be the case—the Senate would make the decision. Nationalists protested that this would make the Senate a dangerous aristocracy, and heated debate ensued. Williamson suggested that both houses should decide, each state having one vote, and then Sherman proposed the compromise that was adopted: in the event of a tie or the lack of a majority, the election would be settled in the House of Representatives, each state delegation having one vote for the purpose (September 4–6).

Thus the constitution of the executive branch, like that of the legislative, gave the states qua states a disproportionate share of power in the partly national, partly federal government—again in keeping with the desires of the middle delegates and contrary to those of the nationalists.

THE EVOLUTION OF THE JUDICIARY—AND THE ROLE OF the middle delegates in its formation—cannot be traced in so clear-cut a fashion. Early on, the Connecticut and South Carolina delegations urged that Congress appoint the judges, against the insistence of Madison, Wilson, and others that the executive appoint them (June 5). They later agreed that the Senate alone should have the power (June 13 and July 21), a position they held until Butler's electoral-college plan was adopted. Rutledge and Sherman opposed the establishment of inferior federal courts, and they were supported by their delegations and by North

Carolina but were opposed by Dickinson (June 5). The Committee of Detail provided that "such inferior Courts as shall, when necessary, from time to time," be established by Congress—meaning that such courts were not mandatory, and implying that they were to be temporary, ad hoc bodies (article II).

The judiciary was subjected to serious discussion on only two occasions. The first was on August 15, when Madison proposed and Wilson seconded a motion that the executive and judicial authorities should be combined for the purpose of vetoing acts of Congress. The Carolinas and Connecticut opposed the motion. Dickinson confessed himself to be perplexed: he rejected the idea of judicial review, but he also, like Sherman, disapproved the notion of mixing executive and judicial powers; and yet some check on the legislative was necessary. The second discussion, on August 27, was more extended: several of the middle delegates made proposals, but they were by no means a cohesive group. Johnson, Dickinson, and Sherman made motions defining and specifying the jurisdiction of the courts, all of which were adopted. Dickinson proposed that judges be removable by the executive on application by Congress, which Sherman supported, Rutledge vehemently opposed, and the convention overwhelmingly rejected, Connecticut alone voting in favor. C. C. Pinckney spoke strongly against Madison's motion to prevent increases in judges' salaries after they had been appointed, and the convention rejected the proposal all but unanimously. It is significant that attendance during this desultory discussion was the lowest of any time during the convention, a bare quorum of seven states having been present for most of the day.

Given such indecisiveness on the issue, Gouverneur Morris took it upon himself—in his capacity as draftsman for the Committee of Style, which put the Constitution into its polished form—to settle the matter according to his own lights. On the subject of the judiciary, he wrote many years later (to Timothy Pickering, December 22, 1814): "Conflicting opinions had been maintained with so much professional astuteness, that it became necessary to select phrases, which expressing my own notions would not alarm others, nor shock their selflove."

But Morris had only the next-to-the-last word. The open-ended language that he employed in Article III left it up to Congress to determine the structure of the judicial branch; the Judiciary Act of 1789 became, for practical purposes, a part of the Constitution. That act was authored by Senator Oliver Ellsworth and was steered through the House of Representatives by Roger Sherman.

ONE MORE BIT OF MANEUVERING WANTS NOTICE. MADison recorded in his journal for August 29 that an understanding had been reached concerning the powers of Congress to interdict the slave trade and to pass "navigation acts"—that is, acts regulating interstate and foreign commerce. The Committee of Detail's draft had prohibited Congress from taxing exports, interfering with the slave trade, and taxing the importation of slaves; and it had required a two-thirds majority in both houses of Congress for the passage of navigation acts. All this had been worked out to the advantage of the Carolinas, presumably with the collusion of Connecticut and in exchange for the Carolinas' support of Connecticut's land claims. Connecticut, having but minimal interest in the import trade and the freight-carrying business, was indifferent in regard to navigation acts, and thus the earlier Carolina-Connecticut bargaining cannot be what Madison referred to on August 29.

Instead, the "understanding" that Madison mentioned must have come about as follows. When the clauses regarding the slave trade and navigation acts were considered on August 22, several delegates voiced strong objections, and the clauses were referred to a special committee.

Two days later the committee reported: Congress could stop the slave trade in 1800, slave imports could be taxed, and navigation acts would require a simple majority. Most delegates from the upper South, which had an excess of slaves, were opposed to the slave trade, and because they feared that northern congressmen would otherwise be able to pass navigation acts that would drive up freight rates, they eagerly supported the two-thirds clause. Apparently, the delegates from South Carolina had then conferred with Sherman, Ellsworth, Nathaniel Gorham of Massachusetts, and John Langdon of New Hampshire to work out an accommodation: South Carolina would oppose the two-thirds rule, and the Yankees would vote to extend the ban against interference with the slave trade from 1800 to 1808 as well as to uphold the ban on export taxes. Whatever the deals, that is the way the participants voted, and that is the way the affected clauses ended up in the Constitution.

But none of this was as important as the structural design of the Constitution. In developing that design, the work of the middle delegates was crucial. It would be going too far, perhaps, to insist that without these eight men the Grand Convention could not have succeeded in its undertaking, though a strong argument could be made for such a proposition. More modestly, it can be said that without the middle delegates the Constitution would have been something quite different—and that it is questionable whether such a constitution would have been ratified.

7
THE CONSTITUTIONAL PRINCIPLES OF ALEXANDER HAMILTON

"MINE IS AN ODD DESTINY," ALEXANDER HAMILTON wrote in 1802. "Perhaps no man in the U States has sacrificed or done more for the present Constitution than myself—and contrary to all my anticipations of its fate, . . . I am still laboring to prop the frail and worthless fabric."

He spoke the truth, without exaggeration. Even as he had signed the document in 1787, he had expressed grave misgivings and had said that he was signing it only because the Constitution offered a "chance of good" and because the alternative was "anarchy and Convulsion." He worked feverishly to bring about its ratification; and once it had been adopted, it was he, more than any other man including Washington, who breathed life into it, who made it into an enduring government. His doubts arose from concern that the Constitution did not provide a central authority strong enough and stable enough to bind together as one nation the intensely provincial American people. His hopes and his labors arose from a belief in the magnificence of the undertaking and from a self-confidence that bordered on the sublime.

The constitutional principles that guided Hamilton in his public career from 1787 onward were the product of interaction between experience and observation, on the one hand, and reading and contemplation on the other. In the pages that follow, we shall attempt to describe that interaction and to show how he applied his principles in the practical business of establishing a viable national government.

HAMILTON WAS A MAN OF ARDENT AND ENTHUSIASTIC temperament, inclined in his thinking to move swiftly and too far in one direction, overreact when he learned the error of his ways, then gradually work back to a firm, balanced position. In his earliest commentary on a written constitution—the New York Constitution of 1777—he belittled the common observation that "instability is inherent in the nature of popular governments." Rather, he insisted, instability arose from mixing the "popular principle" with monarchical and aristocratical principles. "A representative democracy," he added with characteristic self-assurance, "where the right of election is well secured and regulated & the exercise of the legislative, executive and judiciary authorities, is vested in select persons, chosen *really* and not *nominally* by the people, will in my opinion be most likely to be happy, regular and durable." Those thoughts were written in May of 1777; less than a year later, after the bitter winter at Valley Forge, he began to express utter contempt for the people and their representatives, and for a time he was outspokenly elitist. That attitude lasted until the mid 1780s, when close observation of the rivalry between merchants and bankers in New York and Philadelphia demonstrated to him the corrupt behavior that greed could inspire in well-born and generally virtuous men.

Paralleling this zigzag course was Hamilton's changing attitude toward Congress. At first he thought that America "had a representation, that would do honor to any age or nation." By 1778 he was writing that "there is not so much wisdom [in Congress] as there ought to be. . . .

Folly, caprice [and] a want of foresight, comprehension and dignity, characterise the general tenor of their actions. . . . Their conduct . . . is feeble indecisive and improvident." It was at this time that he warmly embraced David Hume's proposition that in framing a government, "every man must be supposed a knave." For a while he also held to the counterpart proposition that men, or at least most men, could be persuaded to act in the public interest only if it were in their private interest to do so. By 1787, however, he had gradually come to a more temperate and judicious understanding, one that would be a polestar during the remainder of his career: public men could be persuaded to act in the public interest by appealing to their reason, prudence, and love of country, provided that so acting was not directly or fatally contrary to their personal interest.

On one subject no evolution of ideas was necessary: the greatest danger to America came from the centrifugal forces that threatened to tear it asunder. From the outset and even when his faith in Congress was at its lowest ebb, Hamilton was convinced that the vital shortcoming in the constitutional order was a lack of power in the central authority and an excess of power in the state governments. He thought that if those arrangements were not drastically altered, they would, soon or late, bring both independence and liberty to an end. At least three times, beginning in 1779, he urged the calling of a convention to increase the powers of Congress. At least twice, once before and once during his tenure as a member of the Confederation Congress, he urged that it simply exercise power without specific constitutional authority, justifying his position on the ground that the responsibilities and duties vested in Congress inherently implied the powers necessary to the fulfillment of those duties.

The intensity of Hamilton's conviction on this matter amounted almost to an obsession, and it is the key to understanding his mature view of the most efficacious constitutional order of the United States. The conviction derived partly from his psyche and his personal history, but it stemmed also from observation. Repeatedly, throughout the war, he saw that Americans were patriotic—that is, were willing to make sacrifices for the good of the nation—whenever British troops were near, but that absent the Redcoats, patriotism was likely to be absent as well. Having no trace of provincialism in his own make-up, he simply could not comprehend it in others. For a time he attributed it, without serious thought, to meanness, spite, envy, greed, and any number of other vices; but in time he came to realize that it had explicable roots and that if he and others were to forge an American nation out of the country's disparate parts, he must explore those roots.

The emergence of his ideas on the subject can be traced in various of his writings between 1783 and 1787, but they are most clearly and fully expressed in his great speech of June 18, 1787, at the Philadelphia Convention. There he posited the proposition that there were five general "principles of civil obedience" which made people loyal adherents to a particular regime, and he elaborated each at some length.

The first was *interest,* by which Hamilton meant the narrow, immediate "active & constant" rewards, whether monetary or psychic, to be derived from supporting a government. He offered as examples New York and other states that had devised "particular plans of finance" to purchase loyalties at the expense of the plans and requisitions of Congress. Similarly, the love of power impelled officeholders in the states "to regain the powers delegated" to Congress, rather than "to part with more, or give effect to what they had parted with." He added that their "esprit de corps"—then a pejorative term—was strong and that "the ambition of their demagogues is known to hate the controul of the Genl. Government."

The second principle was *opinion,* in discussing which Hamilton followed closely the reasoning that David Hume had employed in one of his essays. Hamilton meant the general, usually unarticulated belief that government was necessary and, on the whole, beneficent; in that sense the weight of opinion was solidly on the side of state and local governments. If the Confederation Congress were entirely dissolved, he said, no one would especially miss it, for the particular governments could perform the ordinary functions of government tolerably well, and their capacity to do so would increase over the years. By contrast, most people were of the opinion that a dissolution of the state and local governments would be fatal.

Under the heading of *habit*, the third principle, Hamilton spoke of the "habitual attachment of the people" and their "habitual sense of obligation"; obviously, "the whole force of this tie," historically and presently, was with state and local authority. The sovereignty of the state government, he said, "is immediately before the eyes of the people: its protection is immediately enjoyed by them. From its hand distributive justice, and all those acts which familiarize & endear Govt. to a people, are dispensed to them." Conversely, because "distance has a physical effect upon mens minds" (another Humean conceit), when the unfamiliar and alien general government demanded money or services from the people, they regarded that demand as odious.

The fourth principle was *force*—that is, the coercion of law and the coercion of arms, both of which were necessary. As for the coercive power of law, Congress possessed virtually none, and that of the states was "nearly sufficient," though not entirely so, because law is "inefficient unless the people have the habits of Obedience." As for the force of arms, the states had generally been accustomed to getting along without it, but the experience of Shays' Rebellion had taught that "a certain portion of military force is absolutely necessary in large communities."

Finally, there was what Hamilton called *influence*. He denied that he meant corruption, but his elaboration was scarcely distinguishable from corruption as the term was understood at the time—what would later come to be called patronage. He referred to those regular "honors & emoluments," such plums as militia commissions and judgeships, which "produce an attachment" of the recipients.

In time, Hamilton hoped, it might become possible to turn some of these forces in support of the national government, but for the foreseeable future they would continue to favor loyalty to states, not to the nation. The only way to preserve the Union, therefore, was "to go as far in order to attain stability and permanency, as republican principles will admit."

TO UNDERSTAND HAMILTON'S CONCEPTION OF A WELL-constituted system of government, it is necessary to turn briefly to his emerging perception of himself. As we have seen, it was a convention in eighteenth-century England and America that people in public life and polite society assume a "character," a stylized role that one played or a persona that one wore at all times. Until 1783 Hamilton's character was a military one, that of the officer and gentleman who is rigidly bound by the code of honor and motivated by a craving for glory. Afterward, he restlessly cast about for a larger character that would enable him to win, not mere military glory, but the undying Fame of the Lawgiver.

He found the ideal character, one he could play to perfection, in 1786, when he read Jacques Necker's *Treatise on the Administration of the Finances of France.* In a long introduction to this memoir of his service as France's wartime financial minister, Necker itemized the prerequisites for greatness in a minister of finance, and those qualities matched Hamilton's self-image with mirrorlike precision. Then Necker drew a sketch of the grand things—far grander than any that Hamilton had previously imagined—that an able minister could do. After warning his readers that the game was a perilous one, unfitted for peaceful souls who hoped for serenity in their lives, Necker concluded with a passage that might have been written expressly for Hamilton. "There are men," he wrote, "whose zeal ought not to be cooled: such are those who being conscious that they are qualified for great things, have a noble thirst for glory; who being impelled by the force of their genius, feel themselves too confined within the narrow limits of common occupations; and those, more especially, who being early struck with the idea of the public good, meditate on it, and make it the most important business of their lives. Proceed you, who after silencing self-love find your resemblance in this picture."

Given that conception of his character and given his understanding of the imbalance between centripetal and centrifugal forces in American politics, it became crucial to Hamilton that power—as much as possible, but at minimum the power to tax—be vested in the central government. It would be saying too much to assert that the arrangement and distribution of central power was a matter of indifference to him, but it was nearly so. Unlike Madison and most of the other Framers, Hamilton held no special brief for checks and balances, the separation of powers, or other devices for restraining the general government, for he thought that the states would always be an adequate, and probably more than adequate, source of restraint. He summed up his attitude in *Federalist* number 83: "The truth is that the general GENIUS of a government is all that can be substantially relied upon for permanent effects. Particular provisions, though not altogether useless, have far less virtue and efficacy than are commonly ascribed to them." He summed it up even better in the New York ratifying convention. "Sir, when you have divided and nicely balanced the departments of government; When you have strongly connected the virtue of your rulers with their interest; when, in short, you have rendered your system as perfect as human forms can be; you must place confidence; you must give power." Hence he could labor heroically in the New York Assembly to persuade that body to approve the amendments to the Articles of Confederation, proposed in 1783, that would give Congress an independent source of revenue, and he could do so even as the call for the Philadelphia convention was pending. For he knew in his heart that if the central government had the taxing power and if he could get in a position to manage its finances, he could remake the nation by that means alone.

IT IS FROM THIS PERSPECTIVE THAT HAMILTON'S BEHAVior in the convention can be most meaningfully viewed. As is well known, he was not an especially active member. He arrived on May 18 and served on the three-man rules committee. During the first few weeks of the debates he spoke but little, voting with the advocates of the Randolph Plan but being outvoted in his own delegation by fellow New Yorkers John Lansing and Robert Yates. On June 18 he delivered his great speech, holding the floor all day. As William Samuel Johnson noted, Hamilton's performance was praised by everybody, but his proposals were supported by none. Eleven days later, Hamilton left the convention to attend to private business at home. For various reasons he did not return, except for brief appearances in mid July and on August 13, until September 2. He was instrumental in working out the legal niceties of the provisions for ratification, but otherwise he was generally passive. He was there, as he made clear, only because he wanted to sign the finished document, for he intended to support any plan the convention proposed.

Hamilton would have preferred a constitution more like the one he had proposed in June or like the elaborate version he handed to Madison, the convention's unofficial historian, in September. The democratic branch of his government, though elected for three-year terms, would have been more democratic than the actual House of Representatives, for all free adult males would have been qualified to vote for its members; all other branches would have been chosen by electors and would have served during good behavior. The Senate, not the whole Congress, would have been empowered to declare war, but otherwise Congress would have had power to pass all laws that it deemed "necessary to the common defense and safety and to the general welfare of the Union." The president, however, would have had an unconditional veto, not subject to being overridden. Moreover, the state governors, who would have been appointed by the national government and would have served during good behavior, would have had unconditional vetoes over state legislation.

Hamilton believed that nothing short of these arrangements could ensure that the national government would have sufficient stability and energy to protect itself against the states, which would continue to have most of the "principles of civil obedience" working in their favor. Nonetheless, as indicated, Hamilton resolved to support the Constitution as being better than nothing.

There was more to his decision to champion the Constitution, however, than is evident at first glance. He was aware that the struggle over ratification would in effect be a continuation of the Constitutional Convention because the debates would help shape the original understanding of what the Constitution meant. He was equally aware that the first few sessions of Congress would also be an ongoing convention, because the Constitution left a number of crucial matters to be worked out by the new government. Hamilton flung himself vigorously into both sets of quasi conventions, determined to shape the living Constitution into something more to his liking than the parchment version was.

Hamilton's best-known contribution to the debate over ratification was as coauthor of the *Federalist*. As the prin-

cipal authors, Hamilton and Madison shared many view-
points and objectives, and the essays form a well-rounded
whole; but close analysis reveals profound differences between them. Madison's desire to strengthen the Union
was tempered by concern with guarding against governmental excess. The great difficulty in framing a government, he wrote, was that "you must first enable the government to control the governed; and in the next place
oblige it to control itself." To that end, power must be
divided, and "ambition must be made to check ambition."
Hamilton, by contrast, preferred that power be concentrated as much as circumstances would permit. He argued
that the new government would have powers that inhered
in sovereignty and were limited only by the ends for which
it was created; it would, as he put it, have "an unconfined
authority, as to all those objects which are entrusted to
its management." Thus, for example, he insisted that to
place limits upon the legislative power to provide for the
common defense was "unheard of" and that the power
to tax to promote the general welfare was "indefinite," although his conception of what was encompassed by the
term "general welfare" was itself limited, and quite narrowly at that.

Indeed, Hamilton's often-quoted argument against
a bill of rights, which he set forth in *Federalist* number 84,
is based explicitly upon the recognition that the scope of
federal authority was limited. A bill of rights would be
"far less applicable to a Constitution like that under consideration, which is merely intended to regulate the general political interests of the nation," than to the constitutions of the states, which retained "the regulation of every
species of personal and private concerns." Why, he asked
in regard to the federal Constitution, "should it be said
that the liberty of the press shall not be restrained, when
no power is given by which restrictions may be imposed?"

Among Hamilton's other important arguments in the
Federalist is his justification, in number 78, of the doctrine

of judicial review: the power of the courts to declare that legislative acts or executive actions are void if contrary to the Constitution. To Hamilton this was a matter of logical necessity, not of power, for he believed that the judiciary, having "neither FORCE nor WILL," was "beyond comparison the weakest of the three departments of power." In light of the activism that has characterized the Supreme Court in recent years, Hamilton might seem to have been a poor prophet. But his assertion that the judiciary "can never attack with success either of the other two" branches has proved true: judicial activism has been effective only when directed at states, through the instrumentality of the Fourteenth Amendment.

Yet another argument is less well known—that in number 77 concerning the removal power. Upon careful scrutiny of Article II of the Constitution, Hamilton found, or thought he had found, an oversight that could be a source of the kind of stability and durability that he believed the government would lack. The second section of the article provides that the president shall appoint all high-ranking officials, "with the Advice and Consent of the Senate"; but it makes no provision for removing such officials except through the impeachment process. On the assumption that the power to fire must lie in the hands of those who hire, Hamilton asserted that the consent of the Senate "would be necessary to displace as well as to appoint." He went on to describe how this would contribute to steadiness and permanency in the administration of government: "Where a man in any station had given satisfactory evidence of his fitness for it, a new President would be restrained from attempting a change in favor of a person more agreeable to him, by the apprehension that a discountenance of the Senate might frustrate the attempt, and bring some degree of discredit upon himself." Had Hamilton's interpretation prevailed, a ministerial system, not unlike that evolved in Britain, might well have been the result. The First Congress, however, took the position that the power to remove presidential appointees should reside solely in the president.

Hamilton's role in bringing about ratification of the Constitution in New York can be summarized briefly. Despite the sagacity of Publius, the state's electorate—at which the *Federalist* essays were aimed—voted overwhelmingly to reject the Constitution. In the ratifying convention, Hamilton, John Jay, and Robert R. Livingston advanced a succession of potent arguments in favor of ratification, but to little avail. Hamilton was especially brilliant in countering anti-Federalist objections based upon country-party ideology, such as the fear of standing armies and the need for jury trials in civil cases; but such argumentation won over few if any of the oppositionist delegates. Only after the convention had received the news that New Hampshire and Virginia, the ninth and tenth states, had ratified, meaning that the Constitution would go into effect whether New York approved or rejected it, did the opposition begin to waver; and only after Hamilton and Jay had circulated a rumor that if the state refused to ratify, New York City would secede from the state and would seek to join the Union on its own, did the anti-Federalists capitulate.

IT WAS IN HIS ROLE AS SECRETARY OF THE TREASURY— or as he preferred to think of it, minister of finance—that Hamilton made his greatest contributions toward establishing constitutional government. Those contributions were many and varied, but they may be grouped under three broad headings. The first were administrative. The lifeblood of a government is its capacity to collect and disburse revenue, and almost every detail of the machinery for doing so was established by Congress in accordance with blueprints drawn by Hamilton; he set it in motion, and for more than five years he directed its operations. He had a voice in the affairs of the War Department as

well, being indirectly responsible for paying and supply-
ing the nation's tiny army (for a time, indeed, he doubled
as acting secretary of war); and the peacetime concerns
of the State Department, overseeing international commerce and establishing credit abroad, were also concerns
of the Treasury Department. And on a day-to-day basis,
Hamilton and his subordinates—more than five hundred
civilian employees, as compared with a total of twenty-
two in the other departments—*were* the government; the
president, the Congress, and the courts were on duty only
three or four months each year. Moreover, Hamilton's
operations had to be conducted in such a way as to keep
the Treasury Department above reproach and to avoid of-
fending the tender republican sensibilities of a citizenry
that was accustomed to regard tax collectors as the veriest
enemy of freedom.

The complexity of his tasks and the efficiency with
which he performed them can be seen by considering just
one of his functions, that of making quarterly interest payments on the public debt. About twenty-five thousand
separate transactions were involved. Payments were made
on the first day of January, April, July, and October at the
Treasury and at thirteen state loan offices, scattered over
a thousand-mile area and as much as two weeks' travel
time from the Treasury. There were only six banks in the
country. The main source of revenue was sixty-seven
customs offices, which collected widely varying, season-
ally fluctuating, and often unpredictable sums. But on
interest day, Hamilton had to know how much money was
available, in what places, and in what forms—and had
to move it in appropriate ways. Given the slowness of
communication and transportation, that would seem to
be impossible, and yet during Hamilton's tenure as secretary, there was never once a complaint of error or delay
in the making of interest payments.

Hamilton's second contribution as secretary was to
provide stability during the formative years by causing

the federal government to function as the British ministerial system did, rather than as the Framers had planned,
though always within the framework of the Constitution.
In the British system, as it had evolved under the leadership of Sir Robert Walpole, the king was the symbolic
embodiment of the nation but was not its chief executive
officer: that role was played by the chancellor of the exchequer, who was responsible to king and Parliament but
who acted as the "prime" minister, the person charged
both with the duty of running the government and with
that of setting legislative policy. Hamilton was given the
opportunity to operate the United States government in
that way (though Washington was by no means a mere
figurehead) because the House of Representatives, jealous
of its constitutional authority over money bills and fearful
of executive power, required the secretary of the treasury
to report directly to the House as well as to the president.
It expressly required Hamilton to prepare reports and propose legislation on fiscal policy. That made him, in effect,
a nonvoting member of the House and enabled him to
become the American Walpole.

Hamilton's third, and most enduring, contribution as
secretary was to couple the fate of constitutional government with the development of a free-market economy.
That statement may elicit surprise, for Hamilton did propose, in his "Report on Manufactures," the enactment of
protective tariffs, which are both antithetical to free trade
and also a highly questionable stretching of the Constitution's requirement that taxes be levied only for the common defense and *general* welfare. But the tariffs would
have been minimal and temporary, to last just until certain
industries survived their infancy. Hamilton's larger goal
was as indicated.

The Constitution prohibited the erection of interstate
trade barriers, but economic activity in America was far
from unfettered, as we shall see in a subsequent essay.
Only under the *lex mercatoria*—that is, the established rules

and customs that governed the international exchange of commodities and bills of exchange, notes, and other negotiable instruments—was economic activity free from governmental restraint.

Therein lay the reason for Hamilton's belief that he could bring about fundamental change by the way in which he administered the nation's finances. The *lex mercatoria* was consistent with Hamilton's ideas about liberty, industry, justice, and honor, because it was based upon free but orderly and structured contractual relationships. It governed all international transactions in commercial paper, and by transforming the public debt into the basis for the nation's currency and banking system, Hamilton saw to it that the spirit of the *lex mercatoria* governed that system as well. Because the public debt was huge, being many times the amount of hard money in circulation, to turn the debt into money was to infuse the whole of American society with that spirit.

The genius of Hamilton's program lay in his idea of establishing rules and procedures that would make money the universal measure of the value of things. He constructed efficient fiscal machinery, made it beneficial to everyone, and interlocked its operations with the workings of the economy. It was so designed that the people came, imperceptibly, to find it a convenient, a useful, and finally a necessary part of their daily lives. That accomplished, everyone had to comport himself in accordance with the rules by which the machinery of government itself functioned, and it became almost impossible to dismantle the machinery short of dismantling the whole society. The permanence and stability of the constitutional order had become inescapably connected with a free economic order.

IN ADDITION TO HELPING ESTABLISH CONSTITUTIONAL government through his actions, Hamilton helped shape contemporary and future interpretations of the Constitution through opinions he wrote in various capacities. Some had influence and implications quite as profound as any decision that Chief Justice John Marshall would write. Indeed, at least two of Marshall's major opinions were drawn directly from Hamilton's earlier constitutional pronouncements.

Hamilton's most famous opinion was that of February, 1791, in which he advised President Washington in regard to the constitutionality of the bill to incorporate the Bank of the United States. Secretary of State Thomas Jefferson and Attorney General Edmund Randolph had previously advised the president that the bill was unconstitutional on the ground that the Constitution did not empower Congress to establish corporations (a motion to give Congress that power had, as both Washington and Randolph knew, been explicitly rejected by the Philadelphia Convention). In response, Hamilton formulated the classical expression of the doctrine of implied powers, or the so-called loose construction of the Constitution. Jefferson and Randolph had argued as if the creation of a corporation was an end rather than a means to an end. The real issue, Hamilton insisted, was whether the corporation in question was being erected for a legitimate, constitutional purpose. "If the end be clearly comprehended within any of the specified powers," he said, and "if the measure have an obvious relation to that end, and is not forbidden by any particular provision of the constitution—it may safely be deemed to come within the compass of the national authority." He added several further criteria: the proposed mean must not "abridge a preexisting right of any State, or of any individual," and it must not be "immoral" in itself, or "contrary to the essential ends of political power." Marshall would paraphrase this argument in ruling on the constitutionality of the Second Bank of the United States in *M'Culloch* v. *Maryland*.

As for the contention based upon the refusal of the Philadelphia Convention to grant the power of incorporation, Hamilton offered a common-sense proposition: "Whatever may have been the intention of the framers of a constitution, or of a law, that intention is to be sought for in the instrument itself, according to the usual & established rules of construction. Nothing is more common than for laws to *express* and *effect,* more or less than was intended." Accordingly, if a power to erect a corporation could be fairly deduced from the words of the Constitution, "arguments drawn from extrinsic circumstances, regarding the intention of the convention, must be rejected."

Hamilton's opinions continued to be of influence after he had retired from the Treasury and resumed his law practice. He intended not to practice in the federal courts, for greater challenges and rewards were to be found in state courts. But just after he returned to private station, a group of Virginia Republicans challenged the constitutionality of a tax on carriages that had been levied on Hamilton's recommendation, claiming that it was a direct tax and thus fell within the Constitution's mandate that such taxes must be apportioned among the states in relation to their population. The attorney general of the United States, William Bradford, asked Hamilton to plead the case as special counsel for the government. Hamilton did so, arguing that the tax was actually an excise and need therefore merely be uniform throughout the country. The Supreme Court, in the first case in which it passed upon the constitutionality of an act of Congress, so ruled.

Another opinion was an advisory one. In 1795 the legislature of Georgia granted four companies of land speculators 35 million acres for a paltry $500,000, the inducement being bribes paid to the lawmakers. A year later a rival faction of politicians gained control of the legislature and passed an act rescinding the sale. A former political supporter of Hamilton's, Senator James Gunn of Georgia, headed one of the companies; and another ally, Congressman Robert Goodloe Harper of South Carolina, was attorney for the companies. They sought Hamilton's legal counsel on the controversy, and he responded with a broad interpretation of the contract clause of the Constitution. In Article I, Section 10, states are prohibited from passing any laws "impairing the obligation of contracts." It had previously been assumed that the clause referred only to contracts between individuals, but Hamilton—who may very well have authored the contract clause and with just this in mind—argued that it also applied to contracts between states and individuals, that grants were contracts, and therefore that Georgia's rescinding act was unconstitutional. In 1810, his argument was brought to bear before the Supreme Court in the case of *Fletcher* v. *Peck*, and the Court ruled in accordance with his opinion. It extended that ruling to apply to corporate charters in the Dartmouth College case a few years later, with profound implications for America's economic development.

In a semiofficial capacity, Hamilton dealt with a subject that was to be a hot political and constitutional issue during much of the nineteenth century—namely, that of "internal improvements" at the federal government's expense. While serving as commanding general of the American army during the Quasi War with France, Hamilton wrote to Senator Jonathan Dayton (who had been a member of the Philadelphia Convention), offering a number of suggestions for strengthening the nation's capacity for defense. Among his proposals was the improvement of internal transportation facilities. Congress should, he urged, build an extensive network of roads, which it had the constitutional authority to do under the power to "establish post offices and post roads." He also thought that Congress should authorize the construction of a system of interstate canals to make the inland waterways navigable, but—significantly—he declared that this could be done only if the Constitution were amended.

Possibly Hamilton's most vociferously expressed constitutional opinion was one concerning the federal judiciary. Early in 1801, after Jefferson had been elected president but before he had taken office, the lame-duck Congress passed a revised Judiciary Act which, among other things, created a number of new federal courts. President John Adams filled most of these positions with what Jefferson called "midnight appointments," and the Jeffersonians were outraged. Early in 1802 the new Congress passed an act repealing the Judiciary Act of 1801, thus vacating the new positions. Hamilton argued, in a series of newspaper articles and in an address to the New York City bar association, that the repeal act was clearly unconstitutional, since the Constitution provides that federal judges hold office during good behavior, and the act removed the new judges by legislative fiat. His position was sound, but politics prevailed.

Two years later, Hamilton was counsel in a legal action that did not bear directly upon the Constitution but was pivotal to the whole concept of free and lawful government. Harry Croswell, the printer of a small upstate New York newspaper, ran a story charging that Jefferson had hired a notorious pamphleteer to calumniate Washington and John Adams, "grossly slandering the private characters of men, who, he well knew were virtuous." The charge against Jefferson was true, but Ambrose Spencer, the Jeffersonian attorney general of New York, brought seditious libel proceedings against Croswell and obtained a conviction. Croswell appealed and engaged Hamilton to argue the appeal before the New York Supreme Court.

At issue was the refusal of the trial court to admit as a defense testimony regarding the truth of what Croswell had written. Under the English common law as adopted by New York, truth was not admissible as a defense in cases of seditious libel. Hamilton was concerned with the suitability of that doctrine in a republic, and he set out to have it struck down. Libel, he said, was "a slanderous or ridiculous writing, picture or sign, with a malicious or mischievous design or intent, towards government, magistrates, or individuals." The criminal quality in it was malice, or intent to defame, and truth was relevant to determining intent. Truth was not an absolute defense; it should not be used wantonly, "for the purpose of disturbing the peace of families" or for matters that do not "appertain to official conduct." But he added: "That the truth cannot be material in any respect, is contrary to the nature of things. No tribunal, no codes, no systems can repeal or impair this law of God, for by his eternal laws it is inherent in the nature of things." Hamilton went on to declare: "If you cannot apply this mitigated doctrine for which I speak, to the cases of libels here, you must for ever remain ignorant of what your rulers do. I never can think this ought to be; I never did think the truth was a crime; I am glad the day is come in which it is to be decided; for my soul has ever abhorred the thought, that a free man dare not speak the truth."

The court was divided, and the conviction was allowed to stand; but Hamilton's eloquence was not in vain. Most members of the state legislature came to hear his argument, and a bill was forthwith introduced to declare Hamilton's position the law of the state. It was formally passed the next year, and in time it was embraced throughout the American Republic, forming the legal foundation, firmer than any provided by the First Amendment, for the ideal of a free and responsible press.

Hamilton's last contribution to American constitutional discourse was in the form of an amendment that he proposed in 1802. The Constitution provided that presidential electors be chosen in any manner that the several state legislatures should direct and that electors vote for two candidates; whoever got the most votes (if a majority) would become president, and whoever got the second most would become vice-president. In 1800, most of the electors were chosen by the legislatures themselves, and the electoral votes were equally divided between Jefferson and Burr, with the result that the House of Representatives made the selection. There was widespread sentiment for changing the Constitution to provide that electors vote separately for president and vice-president. Hamilton's amendment would have done that, but it would also have required that electors be chosen by popular vote on a district basis, rather than by legislatures and at large. This democratization of presidential elections would, in Hamilton's view, have provided greater stability by removing the choice from the machinations of politicians. Hamilton's proposal was adopted as a resolution by the New York legislature and then introduced in Congress. It passed in the House but was rejected by the Senate. Subsequently, Congress passed, and the requisite number of states ratified, the Twelfth Amendment, which provided that electors vote separately for president and vice-president but left the method for choosing the electors up to the legislatures.

DISCOURAGED BY FAILURES AND DEPRESSED BY THE RE- peal of the Judiciary Act of 1801 and by other actions of the Jefferson administration, Hamilton feared that the end of constitutional government in America was imminent. In that mood he wrote to his old friend Gouverneur Morris that "the time may ere long arrive when the minds of men will be prepared to make an offer to *recover* the Constitution, but the many cannot now be brought to make a stand for its preservation." It was in the same letter that he spoke of his "odd destiny" and his labors to "prop the frail and worthless fabric." He ended by asking: "What can I do better than withdraw from the Scene? Every day proves to me more and more that this American world was not made for me."

Two years later Hamilton was dead, slain at the age of forty-seven by Aaron Burr. Gouverneur Morris pronounced the eulogy. What Morris said provides a valuable guide for Americans to this good day. "I CHARGE YOU," he declared, "TO PROTECT HIS FAME—It is all he has left—

all that these poor orphan children will inherit from their father. But, my countrymen, that Fame may be a rich treasure to you also. Let it be the test by which to examine those who solicit your favour. Disregarding professions, view their conduct and on a doubtful occasion, ask, *Would Hamilton have done this thing?*"

8

THE CONSTITUTION
AND THE SEPARATION
OF POWERS

THAT THE FOUNDING FATHERS ENDORSED THE DOCTRINE of the separation of powers is taken for granted. "The accumulation of all powers, legislative, executive, and judiciary, in the same hands," said James Madison, echoing Montesquieu, "whether of one, a few, or many, and whether hereditary, self-appointed, or elective, may justly be pronounced the very definition of tyranny." In the Constitutional Convention a wide range of delegates, from the nationalists Gouverneur Morris, Rufus King, and James Wilson to the anti-Federalists Elbridge Gerry, Edmund Randolph, George Mason, and John Francis Mercer, directly or indirectly expressed the idea that separation of powers was indispensable to free government.

That such views precluded the use of the English constitution as a model for American government would seem evident. The eighteenth-century British ministerial system effectively joined the executive and the legislative branches and, through what amounted to the doctrine of positive law, subordinated the judiciary. That system was anathema to the vast majority of Americans: American political rhetoric throughout the last third of the eighteenth century repeatedly attested fear of and hostility toward ministerial government. And yet, as we have seen, Hamilton successfully established a modified version of the ministerial system, and he did so within the framework of the Constitution. The truth is that the Constitution is ambiguous in regard to the relationship between the various branches of government, and the resolution of the ambiguity was left to be worked out by experience.

It is obvious that the Americans gave lip service to the doctrine of the separation of powers. The bill of rights in the Virginia Constitution of 1776 declared that "the legislative, executive and judiciary departments shall be separate and distinct." The Massachusetts Constitution of 1780 was more emphatic: "The legislative department shall never exercise the executive and judicial powers, or either of them: The executive shall never exercise the legislative and judicial powers, or either of them: The judicial shall never exercise the legislative and executive powers, or either of them: to the end it may be a government of laws and not of men."

But if practice, not declamation, be the criterion, it is equally obvious that commitment to the doctrine was actually minimal: every constitution established in the United States prior to 1787 provided for legislative supremacy quite as complete as that of Parliament. The Confederation Congress had neither executive nor judicial branches, and its administrative and judicial agencies were entirely responsible to the unicameral Congress. Every state but one had a single executive, but no executive except the governor of New York had any power to speak of, and the governorship of New York was by no means an independent branch. The state courts, too, were subordinate to the legislatures; the supposed precedents for judicial review, notably the cases of *Rutgers* v. *Waddington* and *Trevett* v. *Weeden*, actually demonstrated the impotence of the courts vis-à-vis the legislatures.

As for the Constitutional Convention, the record is considerably less conclusive than would at first appear. For one thing, it must be remembered that the delegations of three states (New York, New Jersey, and Delaware), along with half of Maryland's, supported the Paterson Plan; and that plan provided for no genuine separation of powers. For another, even among those who voted against the Paterson Plan, some explicitly favored the primacy of the legislative. For instance, Roger Sherman thought the executive should "be appointed by and accountable to" and "absolutely dependent on" the legislative; "an independence of the Executive on the supreme Legislative was in his opinion the very essence of tyranny."

To be sure, this was a minority viewpoint, but the majority itself was divided. The most vigorous advocates of separation of powers sought, not to restrain the federal government, but to strengthen it by removing the executive and judicial branches from the control of a popularly elected legislature. Wilson supported an absolute veto for the president; Charles Pinckney, Gouverneur Morris, and Rufus King proposed that the president not be impeachable. And if these men, who did not fear centralized power, sincerely supported the doctrine of separation, the reverse was true of those who most feared such power: the latter frequently spoke in behalf of the doctrine but were rarely willing to give it their support. John Dickinson and Gunning Bedford, while verbally endorsing the principle of separation, advocated congressional removal of the president on the request of a majority of the state legislatures; Dickinson and John Francis Mercer wanted to forbid the courts the power of judicial review; and Elbridge Gerry objected to the Constitution for the reason, among others, that the judiciary would be "oppressive."

The delegates' mixed feelings are best illustrated by their difficulties in agreeing upon a properly constituted executive branch. Legislative supremacy, or executive accountability to the legislative, is the essence of the ministerial system. Knowing this, the delegates nonetheless so distrusted executive power that until almost the end of the convention, they proposed to make the president a creature of Congress. As the draft constitution stood on September 5, both the executive and judicial branches were mere arms of Congress, the president being elected by the Congress, other executive officers and the judges being appointed by the Senate, and all being subject to removal by Congress. Only when the convention adopted the electoral college did a mixed system, involving some of the principles of separation of powers and checks and balances, fall into place.

Even then, the convention declined to make either the presidency or the courts into fully independent branches. First, of course, Congress was given the power of impeachment. More importantly, though the Constitution vests "the executive power" in the president, it does not specify what that power comprises except by implication. Most of the traditional executive powers, including those of war and peace, the governance of the armed forces, the conduct of relations with foreign governments, the coining of money, and the appointment of judges and administrative officers, are either vested exclusively in Congress or shared with one or both houses of Congress. As for the Supreme Court, congressional power over it was made virtually absolute, inasmuch as Congress can by joint resolution remove almost all cases from its jurisdiction.

In other words, the Framers of the Constitution simply did not provide for a clear-cut separation of powers. Their willingness to go as far as they did stemmed largely from the assumption that George Washington would be the first president and that he could be trusted to flesh out the executive branch in ways that were compatible with the public safety.

WASHINGTON WENT ABOUT HIS DELEGATED TASK WARily. He took seriously his oath of office, and it is to be remembered that the president is the only governmental

official who is constitutionally required to swear to "preserve, protect, and defend the Constitution." Recalling the
debates in the convention, he viewed the veto power as
being designed primarily for that purpose—that is, as a
form of executive review, as opposed to judicial review
of the constitutionality of acts of Congress.

In this and in other matters, Washington tended at
first to read the Constitution literally, almost as a manual
of instructions; and for a time that practice gave him problems. He was a skillful and experienced administrator, but
he could function well only with the help of subordinates
and advisors from whom opinions could be solicited in
full discussion. The Constitution made no provision for
such advisors, and a number of people had opposed its
ratification for that reason. Instead, it merely authorized
the president to require "the Opinion, in writing," of department heads. Washington apparently regarded that as a
restriction, for throughout his first term he adhered to the
practice of soliciting written opinions from his department
heads. This created an enormous amount of paper work
and was far from satisfactory as a way of obtaining advice,
and yet it was not until 1793 that Washington began to hold
regular "cabinet meetings" in which he and the department heads met face-to-face. At first that was even less
satisfactory than the earlier method, for the bitter hostility
between Jefferson and Hamilton made every meeting an
occasion for rancor; nevertheless, such meetings became
an established institution.

In the meantime, Washington had sought two other
prospective sources of advice, neither of which worked
out. The Constitution empowers the president to make
appointments and negotiate treaties with the "Advice and
Consent" of the Senate. When Washington took office, negotiations with various Indian tribes had been under way
for some time, and in 1789 it became necessary to issue
additional instructions to the negotiators. Superintendent
of War Henry Knox asked Washington how to proceed,

and the two agreed that the Constitution required them to seek the advice and consent of the Senate. One Saturday morning, just as the Senate was commencing business, they approached the chambers, asked the doorkeeper to announce their presence, and informed the members that they were there for advice and consent. Knox handed a paper to Washington, who handed it to a nonplussed Vice-President John Adams, who read it aloud. Unfortunately, a number of carriages were just then rolling by on the cobblestone streets, and though the senators caught the word *Indians*, few could make out much else. When the reading was done, Washington said something about seven points regarding which advice and consent was requested, but again outside noises prevented anyone from hearing. After a long and awkward silence, Senator Robert Morris deferentially asked that everything be read again. Everything was read again. Then Adams put the question: "Do you advise and consent?" on each of the seven propositions. On point after point the senators entered into debate and ended up postponing a decision. The president, who was accustomed to dealing with advisors as subordinates, grew visibly irritated. Finally he stood up and declared angrily: "This defeats every purpose of my coming here." The atmosphere calmed, but slowly. After another encounter the following Monday, it was agreed on both sides that thenceforth no formal advice would be sought and that consent would come after, not before, the president had acted.

The circumstances of that decision were trivial, even comical, but the decision itself was an important one. The episode established a model for the conduct of foreign relations: thereafter, Washington initiated foreign policy on his own, seeking no counsel from the Senate. Indeed, he went so far as to appoint Gouverneur Morris minister to the Court of St. James, not only without the Senate's approval but without notifying the Senate. Moreover, ever after, only "weak" presidents, those who entrusted foreign affairs to the secretary of state, worked through the Senate as a matter of course. Every "strong" president, like Washington, has had as little to do with the Senate as possible, working instead through subordinates in the executive branch. (John Adams, among others, believed that the Constitution should be amended to deprive the Senate of any voice in the conduct of foreign affairs; otherwise, he said, the Senate would become a "Junto of Grandees," all competing to become president.)

Quite as importantly, the episode closed off the possibility—which had been left open by the Constitution—that the office of the president itself might evolve into something resembling a prime ministership. Washington, had he chosen, could have made the president a virtual member of the Senate, but he chose otherwise.

The other possible source of advice that Washington explored was the Supreme Court. The occasion arose during the summer of 1793, when the doings of Citizen Edmond Genet threatened to embroil the United States in the wars of the French Revolution. The cabinet was divided, as Jefferson put it, 2½ to 1½ (Knox and Hamilton on one side, Jefferson on the other, and Attorney General Edmund Randolph wavering); a number of vexing problems in international law were involved; Washington had frequently asked Chief Justice John Jay for advice on matters of policy, and Jay had readily complied; and thus turning to the Court seemed a reasonable course. On July 18, accordingly, Jefferson wrote to the Court on behalf of the president, forwarding a list of specific questions. Jay and the associate justices replied early in August, declining to consider the questions on the ground that "the Lines of Separation drawn by the Constitution between the three Departments of government— their being in certain Respects checks on each other—and our being Judges of a Court in the last Resort—are Considerations which afford strong arguments against the Propriety of our extrajudicially deciding the questions alluded to."

Jay's retreat behind the doctrine of the separation of powers was disingenuous. As indicated, he had frequently advised the president. While chief justice, he had served for three years on the Sinking Fund Committee, a purely executive agency whose other members were the three department heads and the attorney general. He had, three months earlier, responded to Hamilton's request for an opinion regarding neutrality by actually drafting a proclamation to be issued in the president's name. He would, less than a year later, accept an executive appointment as minister plenipotentiary to London while retaining his seat on the Court.

The Court's refusal to offer advice on this occasion was prompted by wholly different considerations. Several members of the Court had been complaining about the onerous duty, imposed on the justices by the Judiciary Act of 1789, of traveling from state to state to double as circuit court judges, and in the Pension Act of 1792 Congress added to their chores by requiring them to pass on the claims of wounded veterans of the Revolutionary War. Five of the justices, including Jay, refused to abide by the 1792 act on the plea that the duties it imposed were not judicial in nature and that it was therefore an unconstitutional violation of the principle of the separation of powers. Having taken that stand, members of the Court could scarcely part from it a few months later. Thus it was that an important precedent was established: the Supreme Court does not give advisory opinions to the executive branch.

OTHER MAJOR PRECEDENTS WERE FORTHCOMING. ONE concerned the question whether "the executive Power" comprehends the traditional royal prerogative to issue proclamations that have the force of law, especially in regard to the conduct of foreign affairs. In the spring of 1793, when Genet landed in America, he began licensing privateers to prey upon British shipping, issuing commissions for armed attacks against British Canada and Spanish Louisiana, and compromising American neutrality in other ways. At cabinet meetings and in written opinions, Hamilton argued that the president had the power to issue a proclamation of neutrality and that he should do so forthwith. Jefferson argued to the contrary, but not in the belief that issuing proclamations was unconstitutional as such (Jefferson would issue them himself when he became president). Rather, he insisted that since Congress had the exclusive power to declare war, it necessarily had the exclusive power to declare that the nation was not at war. Washington did issue the proclamation, although not in the form that Jay had drafted it, and the president's language indicates that he intended it to have the force of a legislative enactment. He warned the citizens: "I have given instructions to those officers to whom it belongs to cause prosecutions to be instituted against all persons who shall, within the cognizance of the courts of the United States, violate the law of nations with respect to the powers at war, or any of them."

Another precedent concerned law enforcement. In some instances it was provided by law that state and local officials were to enforce congressional enactments, and the enforcement of customs duties was entrusted to the Coast Guard. Otherwise, reliance was upon the federal courts in actions brought by the attorney general or by federal district attorneys, which meant in practice that the people who on a day-to-day basis were responsible for executing the law were not members of the executive branch at all, but marshals of the federal courts. The marshals were, however, backed up by an executive reserve: when the machinery proved ineffective, the president could (by law) proclaim an insurrection and call out the militia, in which case the president (by constitutional provision) was commander in chief. That happened during the Whiskey Rebellion of 1794.

Still another precedent was established during Washington's last year in office and was occasioned by the House's attempt to claim a share in the treaty-making power. The treaty that Jay negotiated with Great Britain in 1794 had been the subject of considerable agitation. Madison, Albert Gallatin, and other Republican leaders in the House insisted that because the treaty required certain appropriations and involved the regulation of commerce, it could not become part of the supreme law of the land without the concurrence of the House. A faction of Republicans, seeking to derive from the Jay mission political capital that could be employed in the upcoming presidential elections, pushed through a resolution calling for the president to provide the House with copies of all papers relevant to the negotiation of the treaty.

Washington replied with a firm refusal. He told the House that the papers were none of its business, that they were not "relative to any purpose under the cognizance of the House of Representatives, except that of an impeachment; which the resolution has not expressed." Then he lectured the congressmen on the Constitution. Secrecy was sometimes necessary in the conduct of foreign relations, he said, and though that could be dangerous, the Constitution had averted the danger by making the Senate, but not the House, partially privy to such matters. He closed with two telling points: the House had been routinely carrying treaties into effect for seven years without once having asserted a right to do otherwise; and the Constitutional Convention had overwhelmingly rejected a proposal that "no Treaty should be binding on the United States which was not ratified by a Law." That confirmed the original understanding by effectively separating the powers of the Senate from those of the House. Washington's position in the matter went unchallenged for nearly two centuries.

IN A LARGER SENSE, HOWEVER, THE WASHINGTON AD-
ministration's stand on constitutional issues was to be
altered. To republican purists, the administration had been
suspect from the outset, or at least from early 1790, when
Hamilton presented his "First Report on the Public Credit."
Most of the early opponents—Gerry, the dour Pennsyl-
vanian William Maclay, Thomas Sumter of South Carolina,
and the Virginians John Taylor of Caroline, John Page, and
James Monroe—had been anti-Federalists, and few people
took them seriously. But in the spring of 1791 Thomas Jefferson "discovered" that Hamilton was the agent of a
monarchist conspiracy, and the opposition began to take
on formidable proportions.

Jefferson describes in his *Anas* the occasion for his discovery: a dinner party he gave in April of that year. The
secretary of state had supported Hamilton's proposals to
establish public credit and, despite their disagreement
over the constitutionality of the Bank of the United States,
still regarded Hamilton with a friendliness that bordered
on intimacy. Now, Congress was out of session, and Washington had gone on an extended tour of the southern
states, leaving John Adams, Jefferson, and Hamilton together in reasonably relaxed circumstances for the first
time. After dinner the three became engaged in a conversation about political philosophy. The vice-president, in
his customary pontifical fashion, declared that if the British governmental system were purged of its corruption
and if representation in the House of Commons were
made equitable, "it would be the most perfect constitution
ever devised by the wit of man." Jefferson, who recorded
the conversation later, was scarcely pleased to hear his
old friend espouse a government of "two hereditary
branches and an honest elective one"; but he was not
surprised either, for it was well known that Adams had
drifted in that direction. Hamilton's retort, however, shook
Jefferson deeply. "Purge it of its corruption," Hamilton said

casually, "and give to its popular branch equality of representation, and it would become an *impracticable* government: as it stands at present, with all its supposed defects, it is the most perfect government which ever existed." Entirely misunderstanding the remark, Jefferson immediately became convinced that Hamilton had been "bewitched and perverted by the British example" and had formed a "mercenary phalanx" in Congress with a view toward corrupting America, even as his evil idol Walpole had corrupted England.

Forthwith, Jefferson and Madison and a growing number of supporters undertook a republican counterconspiracy to thwart what they saw as Hamilton's monocratic conspiracy. Their strategy, which in its general outlines followed the blueprints laid out by Bolingbroke in his *Idea of a Patriot King* and his *Dissertation upon Parties*, had three parts. First, they would inform Washington of Hamilton's sinister designs and hope that the president, acting as a purely republican "patriot king," would rein in his unfaithful minister and "restore" the Constitution. Secondly, to destroy Hamilton's power over Congress, they would make a determined effort to overcome the "money phalanx" and sever the connection between the legislative branch and the heads of executive departments—which is to say, require Hamilton in future to report only to the president rather than directly to Congress. Third, they would organize a political party. Parties were widely regarded as fatal to good government, and especially to republican government, but Bolingbroke had suggested a kind of party that need not be so. This would be the party of all the people, and it would be the party to end all parties. It would gain control of government, oust the ministers and moneychangers from the temple, restore the Constitution, and then wither away. Such was the Republican party as Jefferson and Madison conceived it.

Based as it was on mutual misunderstanding, the partisan division rapidly widened and led to further misunderstandings. Hamilton and his supporters, laboring diligently to build an energetic, stable, prosperous, and free republic, could perceive the opposition only as the work of artful and designing scoundrels. Congressman Fisher Ames summarized the Hamiltonian view succinctly: the Republicans, he said, "generated a regular, well-disciplined opposition party, whose leaders cry 'liberty,' but mean, as all party leaders do, 'power.' " In the absence of a concept of a loyal opposition (the Jeffersonians' loyalty was sometimes as questionable as Bolingbroke's had been), the Hamiltonians were ready, by 1793, to believe that the Jeffersonians were adherents of an international Jacobin conspiracy. The stakes of the game, Hamilton wrote to a friend in 1795, "may be for nothing less than true liberty, property, order, religion and of course *heads.*"

On the Jeffersonian side, the split was exacerbated by frustration. Fully convinced that theirs was the cause of liberty, republicanism, and the Constitution, they interpreted every setback as evidence of the demonic power of their enemies. And the setbacks were numerous. Washington flatly refused to believe Jefferson's charges against Hamilton. Congress repeatedly exonerated Hamilton of accusations made by Republicans, repeatedly enacted his measure, repeatedly refused to change his special relationship with the House. Nor, despite the energy, money, and organizational skill that the Republicans poured into their effort to build a popular party, were they especially successful at the polls. They failed to gain control of either the presidency or the Congress during the 1790s, and when they finally did triumph in 1801, their victory was accomplished, not through the votes of an aroused electorate, but through backstage manipulations in the state legislatures.

Upon obtaining control of the federal government, the Jeffersonians set out to accomplish what their leader afterward described as the Revolution of 1800. Historians and political scientists have been wont to dismiss that description as hyperbolic, since the transfer of power was not accompanied by violence, bloodshed, or mass arrests; but Jefferson's statement is inaccurate only in its dating, inasmuch as the revolution unfolded between 1801 and 1805. During that period the Jeffersonians set the Hamiltonian fiscal system in train toward early extinction, abolished most domestic taxes, emasculated the armed forces, and repealed various Federalist enactments that they insisted were oppressive and restrictive partisan legislation. It had never been in the nature of government to pay its debts, abolish taxes, voluntarily reduce its power to coerce, and curtail its authority; the Jeffersonians did so, and thereby temporarily reversed the flow of history.

And they effected a constitutional revolution as well. To recapitulate, the Framers had not incorporated the doctrine of separation of powers into the Constitution, in large measure because of fear of an independent executive. Out of the same fear, the First Congress had attempted to make the most important executive department, the Treasury, subordinate to the House rather than to the president, and that gave Hamilton the opportunity to fashion what was in effect a ministerial government. In their reaction against Hamilton's system, the Republicans had sought to induce Washington to "restore" the Constitution by divorcing the executive from the legislative. That failing, they organized a Bolingbrokean party, and when they won the presidency, it became up to Jefferson to "restore" the Constitution. He did so, erecting a wall of institutional separation between the presidency and Congress designed to ensure that no Hamilton-style ministry could arise again.

But there was one shortcoming in the Jeffersonian model of separation of powers. To Jefferson, separation meant separation of presidency, Senate, and House. It did not extend to an independent judiciary; the Jeffersonians attempted to make the federal judiciary, as the only non-elective branch, subordinate to the elective branches. The Federalists resisted mightily, and on March 1, 1805, when they joined a handful of dissident (or constitutionally scrupulous) Republicans to defeat the impeachment of Justice Samuel Chase, the independence of the judiciary was assured. The Marshall Court did the rest.

In sum, the doctrine of the separation of powers was not in the Constitution as originally drafted: the Jeffersonians put it there. More properly, they put three-fourths of it there, and Federalists in retreat added the remaining quarter. Subsequently, the doctrine became enshrined as hallowed tradition, with an unforeseen result. To separate government into distinct and coequal branches was to frustrate the idea of checks and balances and to invite one or another of three things: hostility between the branches, supremacy of one, or impotence. During our history we have had all three, but the most common has been impotence. Whether that is for the better or for the worse is an open question.

9
THE PRESIDENCIES OF GEORGE WASHINGTON AND THOMAS JEFFERSON

THE PRESIDENCIES OF GEORGE WASHINGTON AND Thomas Jefferson were profoundly different. The two men represented mutually hostile parties, their ideologies were poles apart, their administrative methods were studies in contrast, and their styles were strikingly antithetical. Apart from being Virginians, they seemingly had little more in common than their red hair, and even on that score they differed: Washington never appeared in public without a powdered wig, and Jefferson scrupulously disdained that affectation.

If, however, their periods of incumbency are viewed in institutional perspective—if we consider their presidencies not as administrations but as experiences in the office—we are impressed by similarities rather than differences. Moreover, certain inherent characteristics of the presidency itself become manifest.

Crucial among these is that the presidency is dual in character, entailing two sets of functions so different from each other that the ability to perform them is rarely united in a single person. The governmental functions, involving administrative and executive activities or the formulation and implementation of policy, are the most obvious. But there are also ritualistic and ceremonial functions which, though we tend to think of them as being of lesser consequence, are at least as important as the governmental, and possibly a good deal more. Indeed, scholars have often misunderstood the presidency because they have ignored or underestimated the symbolic aspects of the office; and no small number of gifted men failed as president because they did likewise or were adept at one of the functions but not the other.

The duality of the executive branch became evident in colonial and even in precolonial times. Americans derived their perceptions of the executive branch from the English, who unfortunately were not at all gifted in dealing with executive authority. For some centuries before the accession of the Tudors in 1485, the English tried to get along with home-grown kings, and they underwent a succession of rebellions, civil wars, regicides, and usurpations. The Tudors, who were Welsh, not English, provided stability in the Crown until 1603, albeit with a great deal of social, religious, and economic upheaval. Then came the Scottish Stuarts and, along with them, another century of rebellion, civil war, regicide, and revolution. At last, in 1714, the English found a king with whom they could live—George I of the small German principality of Hanover. He understood neither the English government nor the English language, and he spent his reign unhappily wishing that he could return to his beloved fatherland. The Hanoverians have occupied the British throne ever since, down to and including Queen Elizabeth II.

It was under the first two Hanoverians (George I and George II, 1714–60) that the English worked out a permanently viable monarchy. Their solution to their problem was at once ingenious and ingenuous: they divided the royal functions and entrusted them to different persons. Those that had to do with the exercise of power—defending the nation against alien enemies, enforcing domestic order and justice, and deciding upon and carrying out governmental policy—became the province of the ministry, which was composed of members of Parliament and headed by the first lord of the treasury or, if he was a commoner, the chancellor of the exchequer. The ritualistic and ceremonial functions remained the province of the Crown. Removed from the actual work of government, the English Crown became the symbol of the nation, its mystical embodiment, and as such the object of reverence, awe, veneration, and love. George III was a temporary aberration: he attempted, for a time successfully, to reunite the royal functions. Bouts of insanity incapacitated him during much of his reign, however, and during the ensuing Regency the arrangements worked out under the earlier Georges fell quietly back into place. And throughout it all, a people who had formerly been given to rebelling against and even killing their kings remained willing to fight and die for them.

The experience of British-Americans was different, and it led to different futures. Until 1776 the royal or proprietary governors and their councils continued to perform both the ceremonial and the executive functions of their offices, and the adversarial relationship between them and the people, as embodied in their legislative assemblies, continued to reflect the discarded pattern of the English past. Upon the coming of independence, Americans virtually abolished all executive power, only to drift back toward a reluctant recognition of the need for it over the course of the next decade. And as we indicated earlier, the Framers of the Constitution cautiously and with trepidation created the presidency, feeling that it was safe to do so because—and only because—George Washington was available to serve as the first president.

The virtual deification of Washington in his own time, not merely by the multitudes but also by sophisticated and hard-nosed politicians and businessmen, is something of a wonder. Part of the explanation is that he was the nation's military hero, though some other American commanders were abler and had better records. Another part is that he looked like the leader: he was cool and aloof, and tall and powerfully built; and in a country populated mainly by people who were hot-tempered and overly confidential, and short and fat, such attributes were not to be taken lightly. Still another is that he quite self-consciously, and infallibly, played the role of the impeccably upright Father of His Country. And, finally, there was the unspoken (and unspeakable), but nevertheless very real, popular craving for a king.

Therein lay Washington's greatest contribution to the presidency and to the perdurance of republican institutions in America. He provided a halfway house between monarchy and republicanism: he made it possible and safe for Americans to indulge their traditional reverence for the Crown without reneging on the commitment to a republican form of government. The way he played his role was a product of studied design, and he devoted as much time and thought to matters of ceremony as to matters of state. He set a standard of behavior, and so effectively did he comport himself according to it that no less skeptical a person than Abigail Adams, wife of the vice-president and a veteran of receptions at Versailles and the Court of St. James, was almost moon-struck upon meeting the president. She reacted as the Queen of Sheba had when first seeing Solomon: "The half was not told me." Washington, she gushed, moved and handled himself "with a grace, dignity, and ease that leave Royal George far behind him."

As for carrying out the executive functions of government, Washington gradually developed procedures and established means by which responsibilities could be translated into actions, but he was willing to delegate authority and, within limits, to permit a great deal of administrative discretion. He was not a passive or figurehead president, but he scrupulously avoided the formulation of legislative policy, for that, he believed, would have exceeded his constitutional authority: he did not propose specific legislation, and he did not veto bills solely on grounds of policy. On the other hand, he acquiesced in Hamilton's activism on the understanding that the secretary of the treasury was executing the will of the Congress that had created his office.

The Jeffersonian Republicans objected to the Federalists' approach to government on a number of grounds, central among them being the Federalists' conception of the executive. The belief of Jefferson and his followers that Hamilton was a monarchist and the agent of an international monocratic conspiracy was not the only hint of monarchy they detected. They also castigated Washington himself for indulging in royal pageantry and for wallowing, kinglike, in popular adulation. When they came to power, they refashioned the executive in accordance with their ideological precepts.

As for the ceremonial—or what might properly be called the monarchical—functions of the office, Jefferson seemingly rejected them entirely. What he actually did was republicanize them. He ostentatiously foreswore ostentation. He gave no public balls and held no levees, and no one celebrated his birthday. He abandoned the monarchical ritual, which had been followed by Washington and Adams and all state governors, of appearing in person before the legislative branches and afterward exchanging formal messages about the executive message. Instead, when Jefferson had anything to say to Congress, he sent a written note and kept it as brief as possible. He staged no entertainments for the public; instead, his doors were open to all citizens at all times. Finally, he never held "court" for governmental officials or foreign ministers. Instead, he held a continuous succession of small, informal dinner parties, at which the wines were superb and the cuisine was prepared by a French chef, but the atmosphere was one of studied casualness. Unwigged, dressed in frayed homespun and rundown slippers, Jefferson captivated his guests with the folksy, open hospitality of a country squire and with dazzling conversation that ranged from art, architecture, and archeology through mathematics and music to philosophy and zoology.

This was not merely a republican affectation adopted as a counterfoil to aristocratic affectation, nor was it a form of reverse snobbery. Rather, it reflected a calculated design on Jefferson's part, and it accomplished just what he expected it to accomplish. By stripping everyone of the possibility of pretense and the trappings of status, and by dealing with people only in intimate gatherings where he was host and master of the house, he established a setting in which he was utterly without peers. In those circumstances he stood as a tower.

By that means—and through the instrumentality of a well-organized Republican press, which had only to describe him as he truly was—Jefferson became immensely popular. There was, however, a crucial difference between Jefferson's popularity and that of Washington. Whereas Washington had been revered as a demigod and the symbol of the nation, Jefferson made the transition from monarchy to republicanism complete by humanizing the presidency and serving as a symbol, not of the Union, but of the people. That achievement had profound consequences, for as the American people became democratized and spread their society over a vast continent, they sorely needed a symbolic monarch if they were to remain a single nation, and yet they could tolerate one only if he bore the peculiarly democratic stamp that Jefferson had coined.

As to the executive functions, the Republican "Revolution of 1800" took place on several levels and in several stages. Administratively, the government was purged of "irreconcilable monarchists," and in choosing replacements, Jefferson employed an artful blend of patronage and meritocracy. The actual conduct of administration was put mainly in the charge of Secretary of the Treasury Albert Gallatin, who had the twin tasks of dismantling Hamilton's elaborate fiscal machinery and of instituting methodical procedures and strict accounting in place of the slipshod and cavalier ways that had often been followed by the Federalists after Hamilton left office. Gallatin also served as the middleman between the president and Congress. That made it possible for Jefferson to influence legislation without interfering directly in the legislative process and thus to preserve the form of strict separation of powers; and it gave Jefferson all the flexibility of Hamilton's independent ministerial system while it left the president in command.

Jefferson presided over the administration with the easy, relaxed, informal manner that he employed at his White House dinner parties, and with equal success. He conducted cabinet meetings as a democracy of equals, and he allowed Congress to operate with no overt presidential direction and only the gentlest of presidential guidance. Yet until almost the very end, he ran Congress more successfully and more completely than Hamilton had ever done and few succeeding presidents would ever do, and the cabinet always reflected his will except when he had no firm opinions on a matter. Moreover, he did not use the techniques that are often associated with "strong" presidents—popular pressure, naked power, bribery, blackmail, or overt trading. Rather, his achievements flowed from the force of his intellect, his character, and his personality.

But that, perversely, was a grave weakness in the Republican scheme of things: administratively, the system could be made to work only with a Thomas Jefferson at the helm, and so far we have not had another. When Jefferson himself faltered, as he did on several occasions during his presidency, the government almost stopped functioning except in the routine operations of Gallatin's treasury machinery. When Jefferson left the office, the shortcomings of his method of administration rapidly became manifest. The cabinet became the center of petty bickering and continuous cabalizing, and Congress split into irreconcilable factions and repeatedly asserted its will against that of the president.

In other words, Jeffersonians destroyed the English cum Washingtonian-Hamiltonian split system of presidency and erected no viable alternative in its place. The resulting problem has plagued us throughout the nation's history. The most popular presidents in their own times— those who most successfully fulfilled the monarchical function of the office—were such men as Teddy Roosevelt and Jack Kennedy, who obviously put on a good show but never accomplished much of anything, or Andrew Jackson, who won popular adulation while wreaking irreparable destruction. Others were extremely able at getting things done—we make no comment here about the merits of what they were doing, and have in mind such twentieth-century presidents as Taft, Hoover, Johnson, and Nixon—but were so totally incompetent in fulfilling the monarchical function that they were virtually ridden out of the office on a rail. The big winners in the history books are those who—like Lincoln, Wilson, and Truman— were shrewd, devious, unscrupulous, and successful operators, unloved and unlovable in their own times, but whom historians can enshrine as retroactively lovable after all memory of their personalities has disappeared.

The other lessons to be learned from the study of the presidencies of Washington and Jefferson have to do with the exercise, structure, and psychic costs of presidential power in administrations that extend for two terms. The reader will scarcely need reminding that both Washington and Jefferson could have been reelected for a third term, but it must be remembered that it took a great deal of persuasion to get Washington to serve even a second term and that Jefferson announced shortly after his reelection that he would follow Washington's precedent. By Madison's time, the two-term limit had already hardened into tradition.

Given that tradition, the relations between a president

and his party and Congress change dramatically between his first and second terms. Politically they are interdependent during the first term, for each can help the other to reelection. After the president is reelected, they no longer have such a relationship: the president, not coming up for a third election, has no further political need for the congressmen of his party, and he is of no future political use to them. The resulting mutual estrangement is exacerbated by a peculiarity of American political history. That is, although the president is cut off from his power base in government by reason of his lame-duck status, he invariably has the illusion of increased power because he invariably wins more decisively when running for reelection than he did when being elected the first time.

This shifting of political relationships has several major sets of implications. One is that the president's followers, no matter how loyal and honorable they may have been during the first term, tend to start jockeying for positions in the race to become his successor—even though such activity may be inimical to the national interest. Throughout Washington's first term, for instance, Jefferson and Hamilton behaved with some civility toward each other in their roles as secretaries of state and the treasury; during the second term all restraint was abandoned. Hamilton spent almost as much time attacking (or, actually, counterattacking) Jefferson as he did attending to his duties, and eventually he more or less forced Jefferson to resign. Meanwhile, Jefferson neglected his duties in the State Department, attempted to sabotage the administration's foreign policy, and vilified his rival incessantly. Finally, Hamilton's presidential prospects were destroyed by a lurid exposé of his extramarital indiscretion.

A decade later, after Jefferson had been elected for a second term, he was a hapless witness to an even-more-destructive version of the game. His secretary of the navy, supported by factions in the House and the Senate, sought to undermine the administration's foreign policy so as to discredit Secretary of State James Madison as a prospective successor to the presidency. They backed James Monroe, who was then minister to England. Madison, for his part, deliberately hewed to a policy that created a danger of war with Britain, rather than allow Monroe to conclude a treaty that would ensure peace but would also greatly increase Monroe's pretentions to the presidency. Toward the end of Jefferson's second term, the maneuvering for advantage took on extreme proportions: for instance, William Branch Giles of Virginia, who for fifteen years had been an unwaveringly loyal Republican, began to sabotage Gallatin's treasury administration when he learned that Gallatin, instead of Giles himself, might be Madison's choice for secretary of state.

The other implications more directly affect the president and the presidency. The first is that the president, no matter how humble his behavior beforehand, tends to emerge from his triumphant reelection with a sense of power that borders on arrogance, if indeed he does not suffer delusions that he is Superman. To a generation that has witnessed the presidencies of Lyndon Baines Johnson and Richard Milhous Nixon, such an observation will hardly elicit a raised eyebrow; but it may come as a surprise that Washington and Jefferson, in their second terms, also tended to set themselves above the law and to regard opposition or even criticism as being tantamount to treason. Their doing so is understandable in light of the lack of a solid tradition of loyal opposition; still, the phenomenon is indigenous to the office.

Washington, shortly after his reelection, was faced with mounting criticism from informal oppositionist political clubs called Democratic-Republican societies. He regarded the societies much as the late Senator Joseph R. McCarthy regarded "cells" of the American Communist party—namely, as agents of a foreign power and of an international revolutionary conspiracy—but he was at first unable to suppress them. Then a group of moonshiners in the mountains of Pennsylvania besieged and burned the house of a collector of the federal excise tax on whiskey, and Washington proclaimed the action to be the handiwork of Jacobin subversives, the Democratic-Republican societies. He assembled a force of 12,950 militiamen and personally marched at their head to crush the insurrection. That episode typified his attitude toward political opposition during his second administration.

But if Washington's second administration was intolerant, that of the Father of American Liberty, Thomas Jefferson, was a nightmare of repression. Having, after his re-election but before his reinauguration, attempted to have the Supreme Court purged of Federalists through impeachment on purely political grounds, Jefferson went on to sanction the suspension of habeas corpus, the wholesale arrest of citizens without charges, and the forcible removal of accused persons from the vicinage in which they had a constitutional right to trial; he declared large regions in insurrection and under martial law for the legal violations of a handful of persons; he became the only president prior to modern times to by-pass the courts and use the army in the routine enforcement of the laws; he sought, received, and enforced legislation that deprived whole classes of people of their property, not only without due process of law but also without the possibility of a trial; he denounced a critical press with an almost paranoid sense of persecution and attempted, by legal and extralegal means, to suppress newspapers that opposed him.

In the face of all this, his party became split into two ideological wings. One, concentrated in the House and led by John Randolph of Roanoke, veered to the extreme position of the doctrinaire libertarian who would abide the subversion of government and of society itself before willfully jeopardizing the rights and liberties of a single citizen. The other, concentrated in the Senate and led by Giles, reverted to a form of totalitarian republicanism: believing that government in their hands was dedicated to preserving human liberty, they saw legal protection of the civil rights of accused persons as subterfuges behind which traitors and other enemies of liberty could hide. Jefferson almost uniformly sided with this latter group. Among the fruits of their labors was a bill, passed by the Senate but rejected by the House, that would have prescribed the death penalty for any person who "resisted the general execution of any public law."

A second implication of the reelection-and-lame-duck syndrome is related to the first. It is in the nature of the presidency that matters of domestic reform, however engrossing they may be initially, lose their appeal after a time. The chore of manipulating or currying favor with congressmen, necessary though it is, grows tedious and demeaning; and the attraction of dealing with foreign affairs, wherein one has a much freer hand, becomes well-nigh irresistible. So it was with Washington by the winter of 1792/93, and so it was with Jefferson by the winter of 1804/5. Each man found the prospect of close future dealings with Congress distasteful, to say the least; and neither would have been human if, in the afterglow of reelection, a voice deep inside had not whispered that he had now earned the right to stand above that sort of thing.

In any event, though neither of them plunged totally into overseas adventuring upon being reinaugurated—as many of their successors were wont to do—both neglected domestic reform for the sake of foreign affairs in their second terms. Since we are not concerned here with the history of their administrations, but with generalizations about the presidency that can be drawn from them, we shall not dwell on this subject overmuch. It is germane, however, to point out that Washington was more successful in handling foreign relations than Jefferson was, and to suggest a reason. Washington was governed exclusively by his conception of the national interest; Jefferson tempered his policy with considerations of ideology. Historians have generally held that Jefferson's approach was the more progressive, enlightened, and humane and that it was merely bad fortune that his policy brought failure, economic collapse, and ultimately war, whereas Washington's had brought peace and prosperity. That judgment is unfounded. To the extent that ideology, not interest, governs a nation's policy, the nation sacrifices its ability to compromise, to admit it was wrong, and to change. The Jeffersonians were unable to accommodate national interest when it conflicted with their ideology, and thereby they locked themselves into a foreign-policy straight jacket. The inexorable result was Jefferson's calamitous last year in office—wherein, to avoid war in Europe, the United States government virtually waged war against its own citizens.

Still another aspect of the problem is that during his second term the president becomes fair prey for every manner of vilification. Once the reality of his lame-duck status begins to penetrate the popular consciousness, press and politicos move in like hyenas gathering around a wounded lion. It has been so since the beginning. Washington, who had been utterly sacrosanct before, had scarcely been reelected when the personal attacks began. Early in 1793, Philip Freneau's *National Gazette*—an opposition newspaper that was subsidized by Jefferson out of State Department funds—opened the barrage by describing the celebration of Washington's birthday as a "monarchical farce" and by sneering that his sycophants fawned upon him as if he were "Virtue's self." The attacks mounted in shrillness and intensity, and by the end of the year, a New York Republican journal was emboldened to charge that Washington's education had consisted mainly of "gambling, reveling, horseracing and horse whipping," that he was "infamously niggardly" in private dealings, and that despite his pretended religious piety, he was a "most horrid swearer and blasphemer." Before long, if John Adams's recollections are to be believed, "ten thousand people in the streets of Philadelphia, day after day, threatened to drag Washington out of his house, and effect a revolution in the government." For the next two years, as the attacks continued—Washington was accused of stealing from the Treasury and even of having secretly been a traitor during the Revolution—he repeatedly interrupted cabinet meetings to indulge himself in tirades against the press or in fits of self-pity. When he finally left office, Benjamin Franklin Bache—a grandson of Franklin's who was editor of the *Aurora* (Philadelphia)—penned this stirring eulogy: "If ever there was a period for rejoicing, this is the moment. Every heart in unison with the freedom and happiness of the people ought to beat high with exultation that the name of Washington from this day ceases to give a currency to political iniquity and to legalized corruption."

Jefferson's story was somewhat different, for he had been exposed to juicy scurrility throughout much of his public career. Already before he became president, he had been widely castigated as an atheist, a coward, a bloodthirsty revolutionary, a hypocrite, a liar, a demagogue, and a fop; during his first term his improper advances toward the wife of a close friend were revealed in the newspapers; and it was charged (or exposed, depending upon which historians you believe) that he had long had a slave as a concubine and had sired several children by her. Throughout all this, however, he maintained his aplomb and, at least publicly, maintained his posture as the unqualified champion of freedom of the press.

It was during the second term that newspaper attacks finally and deeply began to wound Jefferson—or, to put it another way, that his critics became so vicious that they were at last able to find his vulnerable spots. Curiously, he proved to be relatively insensitive to attacks on his personal behavior or morality but hypersensitive to charges regarding his public conduct; charges that he was an agent or lackey of Napoleon, that he was excessively secretive, or that he dictated to Congress sent him into fits of anger or bouts of depression. His enemies, once they got the knife in, twisted it unmercifully. His response was much the same as Washington's had been, except perhaps that it was more so. He had once written that a free press was more vital to public happiness than was good government and that faced with a mutually exclusive choice, he would readily opt for the press. Now he reinvigorated the doctrine of common-law indictment for seditious libel and attempted to whip the press into line by instituting what he called "a few wholesome prosecutions." That failing to stop the onslaught, he could only fulminate and whimper and rage. "Nothing can now be believed which is seen in a newspaper," he wrote again and again. He remarked repeatedly that it was a "melancholy truth" that supression of the press would be no worse than the press's own "abandoned prostitution to falsehood." He wailed that "our printers ravin on the agonies of their victims, as wolves do on the blood of the lamb."

Along with attacks by the press, there is usually, toward the end, some sort of open rebellion by Congress. This does not always apply, but it is the norm with strong presidents. During Andrew Jackson's last year in office and in Theodore Roosevelt's as well, Congress resolved that it would not receive any further messages from the president. Usually the congressional rebellion emanates from the Senate, which is attempting to regain some of the influence in the conduct of foreign relations which it believes the president has usurped from it. The phenomenon can work with either or both houses, however, and the presidencies of Washington and Jefferson offer illustrations of each of the possible combinations.

With Washington, as we have seen, the challenge was the demand by the House for the papers of the Jay mission, and he was able to thwart it; Jefferson, for his part, did not fare as well. During the last congressional session of his presidency, the Senate rose to reassert its claim to a role in foreign affairs, with a view toward preventing Jefferson's successor from having a free hand in continuing Jefferson's policies. Then both houses decided to scuttle the embargo, on which Jefferson had staked his all as an instrument of foreign policy, and they did so in a way that was at least partly a deliberate insult: they voted that the embargo should expire on March 4; Jefferson's presidency and his favorite policy would die together. Finally, the Senate acted in a manner of calculated cruelty aimed at the fallen president. Some months earlier, Jefferson had appointed an old friend, William Short, to a legally nonexistent post as minister to Russia, expecting that the Senate would routinely confirm the appointment and thus support a pet project that he had long espoused, the opening of diplomatic relations with Tsar Alexander I. For political reasons, Jefferson held back an announcement of the appointment until the last minute. When the senators received it, they summarily and unanimously rejected it.

Given all that has been said, our final point should be obvious. It is that the burden of presidential power over a period of two terms—the psychic cost of the office—is greater than any reasonable man can be expected to bear.

The presidency left Washington a broken and beaten man: embittered, given to rages, and convinced that a conspiracy had undermined his presidency and was hounding him to his grave. Perhaps the most telling testimony as to what the office had cost him is the self-pitying draft of a final message that he composed early in 1796—that is, before Hamilton wrote for him the immortal document that was actually released as his Farewell Address. This is how Washington's original version read: "As this address, fellow citizens will be the last I shall ever make to you, and as some of the gazettes of the United States have teemed with all the invective that disappointment, ignorance of facts, and malicious falsehoods could invent, to misrepresent my politics and affections—to wound my reputation and feelings—and to weaken, if not entirely destroy, the confidence you have been pleased to repose in me; it might be expected at the parting scene of my public life that I should take some notice of such virulent abuse. But, as heretofore, I shall pass them over in utter silence." What followed was an itemized denial of the charges.

And if Washington's presidency ended in anguish, Jefferson's ended in agony. Jefferson had remarked that Washington suffered during his second term "more than any person I ever yet met with," but Jefferson's suffering in the same circumstances was greater. He came to regard each session of Congress as an unbearable ordeal; he repeatedly referred to the presidency as his prison; during his last two years in office he was afflicted with migraine headaches that kept him shut alone in a darkened room for weeks on end; and during his final year he collapsed under what used to be called a nervous breakdown—a total paralysis of will. At last the ordeal was over. On March 4, 1809, he stood at Madison's side while Chief Justice John Marshall administered the oath of office. Jefferson remained in Washington a week, packing his belongings, before quitting the place forever. Then the sixty-five-year-old former president rode on horseback through a snow storm for three days and nights until he regained the sanctuary of Monticello. During the seventeen years that remained of his life, he never again left the foothills of the Blue Ridge Mountains.

CAPITALISM AND
THE CONSTITUTION

AMONG THE MISTAKES HISTORIANS TEND TO MAKE WHEN seeking to understand the past is the judging of intentions from results. Thus, when we observe that a liberal economic order rapidly began to emerge upon the adoption of the Constitution, we conclude rather too easily that the authors of the Constitution had such an order in mind. In reality, the kind of economic order that the Framers contemplated is a subtle and complex question. To be sure, they clearly regarded private-property rights as sacrosanct and regarded the protection of such rights as a primary purpose of government. John Locke, whose views were familiar to virtually every American of the founding generation, had taught that the ownership of property was a God-given natural right, antecedent to civil society; and the Revolutionary state constitutions and bills of rights had given ringing approval to that dictum. James Madison, in the Constitutional Convention, cited "the security of property" as being first among "the primary objects of civil society," and other delegates echoed that sentiment.

But one cannot leap from the Framers' belief in the sanctity of private property to the conclusion that they advocated either capitalism or a free-market economy. The emergence of capitalism required a good deal more than legal recognition of private-property rights. After all, private property had existed under feudalism; indeed, in the economic sense, feudalism can be defined as a system of inherited property relationships, protecting equally the (unequal) private rights of all. For property to be capital it must be employed as capital, which is to say it must be used for the purpose of creating more property. For capitalism to come into being, certain conditions, institutions, values, and circumstances had to come into being beforehand. First was a set of attitudes toward property: that it be freely transferable from one owner to another, that there be no discrimination against commercial property in favor of land, and that active development be socially preferred to passive enjoyment. In addition, capitalism required at least four other conditions: a general commitment to the proposition that economic growth is both possible and desirable, governmental sanction of private endeavor as the principal instrument of growth, recognition of the market as the prime determinant of economic value, and legal and institutional means of turning credit into money and capital.

These conditions were only beginning to exist during the 1780s, when the Constitution was adopted. Granted, broad and general forces had been moving America in a capitalistic direction for a long time. Between 1697 and 1774 the volume of trade between Britain and its mainland colonies had increased tenfold, and despite parliamentary enactments that trade had been carried on with minimal restraint by government. And yet, the post-Revolutionary period was still one of transition from ancient, zero-sum conceptions of economic activity to modern, growth-oriented conceptions. Precapitalistic values, attitudes, and institutions, rooted in the feudal past, were far from dead in America; and those of mercantilism—a system in which economic activity was regulated by the state as a means of aggrandizing the state—were in full bloom. The new values, which looked to free trade, entrepreneurship, and a market economy, were little more than a gleam in the eyes of a few advanced thinkers.

In the evolution of systems of political economy, the significance of the establishment of the Constitution was that it made possible—although it was neither designed to, nor did it, make inevitable—the transformation from the old order to the new.

THOUGH IT IS CLEAR THAT AMERICANS OF THE REVOLU-tionary generation regarded "private-property rights" as morally beyond the reach of government, it is not so clear what they meant by the term. Most would have approved Sir William Blackstone's celebrated definition: "that sole and despotic dominion which one man claims and exercises over the external things of the world, in total exclusion of the right of any other individual in the universe." Neither in law nor in practice, however, was the matter so simple. The right of property is not a single right but an intricate combination of many rights, powers, and duties, distributed among individuals, society, and the state. Blackstone, after formulating his definition on the second page of book 2 of the *Commentaries on the Laws of England*, devotes the remaining 518 pages of the book to qualifying and specifying exceptions to it. Americans, like Englishmen, recognized that a condition of the very acquisition of private property was the subjection of that property to the many rights reserved by "the public," both in its capacity as an aggregate of individuals and in its corporate or governmental capacity.

Moreover, American attitudes and institutions were biased against "capitalism" in crucial ways. One was that personal property, in most of its forms, was treated as distinctly inferior to "real" property in the form of land. The negotiability of personal notes, for instance, was not fully recognized in the law; insurance law was virtually nonexistent; laws against "usury," narrowly defined, obtained in every state. These were not mere matters of oversight, to be rectified routinely in the course of time. Instead, they were reflections of an inherited tradition and of deep-seated popular hostility to all "paper" property, including money and stock. John Adams expressed a widespread attitude when he wrote: "Credit has been the Inlet to most of the Luxury & Folly which has yet infected our People. He who could devise a method to abolish it forever, would deserve a Statue to his Memory."

Another set of obstacles arose from the agrarian tradition and the mystique of the land. Jefferson's oft-quoted opinion—"Those who labor in the earth are the chosen people of God if ever He had a chosen people, in whose breasts He has made His peculiar deposit for substantial and genuine virtue"—was widely shared in America, as was its concomitant horror of the urbanization that attends economic growth: "The mobs of great cities add just so much to the support of pure government, as sores do to the strength of the human body." These prejudices found expression in a variety of ways. Land law itself was tilted against development, the basic assumption being that land was not a productive asset to be used for creating wealth but a private estate to be held for sustenance and enjoyment. Furthermore, the ubiquitous landed-property qualifications for the suffrage and the larger such requirements for officeholders ensured that state and local governments would be dominated by the landed interest, not the commercial, manufacturing, or financial.

Now, it has been pointed out by Joyce Appleby and other scholars that American farmers, even (or perhaps especially) the slave-owning plantation gentry, were commercial producers who raised crops for sale at a profit in international markets and that they sought avidly to expand those markets. But it must be understood that planters rarely—George Washington being a conspicuous exception—sought to maximize production and minimize costs, which is to say maximize profits in order to become able to expand their productive capacity still further. Rather, what they wanted to maximize was their capacity to consume, both directly and through the lavish hospitality that established and confirmed their status. It is significant that John Taylor of Caroline, possibly the most influential southern political economist, regarded consumption as the one true measure of wealth. It is also significant that among southern agrarians, land speculation—which diverted capital, in a capital-starved country, away from productive investment—was the socially acceptable quick route to wealth. None of this is the stuff of which capitalism is made.

That brings us to another attitude necessary for the emergence of capitalism—namely, a general belief in the possibility and desirability of economic growth. On this subject, Americans were of two minds. A mania for "projects" and "improvements," as they were called, had swept Britain early in the eighteenth century and had reached America by the 1780s. And yet, as Alexander Hamilton's survey of the economy in 1791 made abundantly evident, the number of Americans who were actually engaged in developmental activity was minuscule. In the interior of New England and throughout the area south and west of Philadelphia, except for the chartering of two canal companies and the experiments of a handful of gentlemen farmers, the spirit of improvement was simply not in evidence, and most of the people were characterized by what Hamilton called "constitutional indolence."

What is more, the idea of economic growth, with its attendant spread of luxury and economic inequality, was incompatible with a republican form of government, as that form was generally understood. Plato, believing that a relative equality of property was necessary in a republic, recommended that republics not be situated on navigable water, lest trade be encouraged. Lycurgus, in what Montesquieu described as "the most perfect model of government that was ever framed," that of ancient Sparta, banished trade entirely. And as we have seen, Montesquieu himself insisted that all forms of economic activity must be rigidly regulated to preserve the frugality, simplicity, and "mediocrity" of "abilities and fortunes" which were necessary to sustain the public virtue that was the life-giving principle of republics.

Quite as importantly, development was handicapped by the fact that most Americans did not believe economic growth was really possible. Most conceived of economic life as John Adams did, namely as a zero-sum game in which the world's supply of wealth was essentially fixed. One man or one nation, it was generally believed, might obtain a larger share of that wealth, but only at the expense of another man or another nation. Benjamin Franklin, who did not agree with Adams on many things, nonetheless shared that attitude. He characterized all commerce as "generally *cheating*" and wrote bitterly of its corrupting and debilitating effects. Of Americans who wanted to forsake the simple life for the riches of manufacturing and trade, he said: "I can put them in a way to obtain a Share of it. Let them with three fourths of the People of Ireland, live the Year round on Potatoes and Butter milk, without Shirts, then may their Merchants export Beef, Butter, and Linnen. Let them, with the Generality of the Common People of Scotland go Barefoot, then may they make large Exports in Shoes and Stockings: And if they will be content to wear Rags like the Spinners and Weavers of England, they may make Cloths and Stuffs for all Parts of the World."

A small group of Americans, which included Thomas Jefferson, did subscribe to the theories of the French physiocrats, who held that economic growth was possible— but only through work on the land, which they regarded as the sole real source of wealth. Yet physiocratic theory, when coupled with prevailing ideology, was not merely precapitalistic; it was decidedly anticapitalistic. Profits from commerce and manufacturing were reckoned as adding nothing to the value of things but as being stolen from the true producers and rightful owners, those who labor in the earth. Adam Smith, of course, had shown that economic growth was possible, but his work was recent and was by no means universally accepted. Besides, one must remember that even Smith regarded economic "progress" as a mixed blessing. Smith's well-known example of the increased productivity resulting from the division of labor in a pin factory is counterbalanced by the appalling picture he drew of the consequences for factory workers. Every worker "becomes as stupid and ignorant as it is possible for a human creature to become." They are the worst of citizens, and yet "in every improved and civilized society this is the state into which . . . the great body of the people, must necessarily fall, unless government takes some pains to prevent it." Indeed, Smith's gloomy picture of life in an industrialized world and his hostility toward public debt helped prepare Americans to be hostile toward the few who—like Hamilton and Robert Morris—actively labored to bring a dynamic, growth-oriented economic order into being.

Furthermore, the practice of measuring economic value freely in the marketplace existed only to a limited extent in America. It is true that the prices of most goods moving in international and interstate commerce were free to respond to fluctuations in demand and that most land could be bought and sold as a commodity. But the price of bread was normally set by assize; rates charged by millers, ferrymen, wagoners, innkeepers, and operators of other "public utilities" were fixed by law; marketing practices were regulated by laws prohibiting "offenses against public trade," such as forestalling, regrating, and engrossing; and mercantilist codes required the inspection of many goods and prohibited, taxed, or gave bounties to others. Beyond all that, legislatures felt free to interfere in buying, selling, and lending operations even after transactions had been consummated. Patrick Henry expressed a common American disdain for the free operation of the market when he declared that "there are thousands and thousands of contracts, whereof equity forbids an exact literal performance."

Underlying arbitrary governmental interference in the market was an archaic concept of the contract based upon the medieval ideal of "the inherent justice or fairness of an exchange," which in turn rested upon the notion that everything had an intrinsic "fair value" and therefore a "just price." In England, William Murray (Lord Mansfield), in his capacity as chief justice of the Court of the King's Bench from 1756 to 1788, had wrought a revolution that had wrenched English law from its medieval, land-centered roots and transformed it to a code well calculated to facilitate free commercial intercourse. Among other things he reshaped the laws of promissory notes, bills of exchange, bank drafts, and contracts to make them flexible and responsive to the market; and he established the new field of marine insurance. By the time he was done, the *lex mercatoria* had been systematized and made into a pervasive part of the domestic law of Great Britain. And by the 1780s, a modern market definition of contract had triumphed: "It is the consent of parties alone, that fixes the just price of any thing, without reference to the nature of things themselves, or to their intrinsic value."

That construction was widely known in America, but it had not been established in any American jurisdiction. South of the Potomac and in much of New England disapproval was widespread, not least because Mansfield had, as a necessary means to his end, contrived a number of devices for circumventing juries in civil cases—a practice that, as one Virginian put it, did not "accord with the free institutions of this country." As long as juries could decide the law, the legal changes necessary for the triumph of capitalism could not take place; and Americans guarded the prerogatives of their juries jealously.

Finally, the emergence of capitalism required institutional means of monetizing credit. Those means were not only lacking; they were, under existing arrangements, prevented from developing. Quite in addition, there was a mental barrier among merchants, the people whose need for credit was most immediate. To them, credit was personal and a matter of "respectability." Given good family connections, recommendations, and a reputation for integrity, credit was forthcoming even in the absence of collateral. Otherwise it was not. It was ingrained among eighteenth-century merchants to regard as unacceptable the kind of depersonalized, collateral-based credit that is essential to capitalistic enterprise.

For all these reasons, Americans had been unable to develop a workable system whereby future expectations could be turned into money. Few, indeed, had given the matter any serious consideration, though the materials for creating such a system had been at hand since the war. Those materials were in the form of the Revolutionary War debts—about $75 million of assorted securities, unsupported and circulating at ten to twenty-five cents on the dollar. The know-how for using public debt as the basis of private credit and currency was readily available: one could study the examples of the Netherlands and England, or one could read the works of Sir James Steuart. Not many Americans were thinking along those lines, however, and in any event there was no central government with the taxing power necessary to make an adaptation of the Dutch and English systems work in America. Consequently, the public debt was a public burden, crushing the economic activity of which it could have been the life's blood.

IT IS UNNECESSARY, FOR PRESENT PURPOSES, TO INQUIRE whether the Framers of the Constitution intended to change all this and bring about a new economic order. Some did; some did not. The relevant fact is that the adoption of the Constitution made the transformation possible.

Broadly speaking, those features of the Constitution which bear upon the question are of two general descriptions. One group of provisions is specific, being built directly into the instrument; other provisions, those establishing the rules for the levying of taxes and the servicing of public debts, are more open-ended.

Several of the specific features of the Constitution are tilted strongly in favor of a free-market system. One consists of the clauses that made the United States the largest area of free trade, meaning trade unimpeded by tariff barriers or other restrictions, in the world. Others include the prohibition of the taxing of exports and those provisions that empower Congress to establish uniform weights and measures. Equally important was the rejection by the convention, over the protests of the Old Republican from Virginia, George Mason, of a proposal to give Congress power to enact sumptuary legislation. The most important specific provisions are those in Article I, Section 10, which restrict the powers of the states. Some of the prohibitions are political rather than economic, but the crucial clause in the section, and the one that pointed the United States most directly toward a capitalistic future, is the contract clause: No state shall pass any law "impairing the Obligation of Contracts." If it be read broadly, literally, unequivocally, and without regard to the context of the times, the contract clause alone would seem to indicate that the Founding Fathers rejected the existing economic order and endorsed the order that was to come. How they meant it to be read, however, is far from self-evident, as is made apparent by the debates in the convention (see especially discussions on August 28 and August 29). Indeed, two full generations of adjudication would be required to establish a free-market-oriented interpretation of the contract clause, and not until after the Supreme Court's decision in the *Dartmouth College* case (1818) was it interpreted as protecting corporations.

As for provisions concerning the taxing power, those

evolved in the convention with surprisingly little friction. With a minimum of discord, the delegates agreed to vest Congress with a full range of taxing powers, limited only by the requirements that taxes be levied solely for national purposes, that they be uniform, and that direct taxes be proportionate to population. The prohibition of state taxes on imports and exports also met with little resistance, the prohibition of congressional taxes on exports a bit more.

Agreement on provision for the public debts was far less readily attained. Each time the issue was debated, divisions became apparent, and charges were hurled against "Blood-suckers" and "speculators" and the like. Finally, to cool the tempers that had been raised, Edmund Randolph of Virginia proposed the neutral wording that, with minor modifications, was approved in the finished Constitution: "All Debts contracted and Engagements entered into, before the Adoption of this Constitution, shall be as valid against the United States under this Constitution, as under the Confederation."

That passed the buck to the First Congress, which—under Hamilton's leadership—seized it boldly. Whatever the intentions of the Framers of the Constitution may have been, Congress made the commitment to capitalism complete. Within the framework of a limited government, under law, the United States would develop an economic order regulated mainly by the market and driven mainly by private enterprise for personal profit.

It is possible to denigrate the society that resulted as being one of grubby, materialistic, self-seeking acquisitive individualists, but to do so is totally to misunderstand the genius of the American experiment. As Henry Adams put it, the ordinary European looked at the overcivilized Old World and saw it as a hopeless vale of tears; the ordinary American looked at a raw wilderness and saw it as boundless fields of grain and thriving communities that he and his children and his children's children would make: and in that sense, the American was the most idealistic man on earth.

In any event, the American system of political economy worked for a long time—actually until the 1960s—and along the way the United States became the freest, richest, most generous, and most powerful nation in the history of the world. Then came a sadder story, but that lies beyond the scope of this paper.

Let us conclude simply. The Framers of the Constitution may or may not have intended that this should have become a capitalistic society, but constitutional government and capitalism became inextricably intertwined at the outset. They were born together, they grew up together, they prospered together, and—unless we return to limited government under law and soon—they will die together.

II

FEDERALISM IN AMERICA:
AN OBITUARY

A CENTRAL FEATURE OF THE NEW ORDER THAT WAS
created in Philadelphia in 1787—perhaps the central feature—was federalism, which in America has historically
had three distinct dimensions. The first is the representation of the states as states in the national government: what
James Madison had in mind when he wrote in *Federalist*
number 39 that the Constitution established a system that
was partly national and partly federal. The second involves
the source of sovereignty in America and the nature of the
constitutional union. The third, and ultimately the most
important, has to do with the division of the powers of
sovereignty between national and state governments.

In each of these dimensions federalism has a separate
history, but the end result has been the same. For many
years, the system served as a protector of liberty and a
preserver of local autonomy, as the authors of the Constitution intended. Over the course of time, however, federalism in each of its aspects has been undermined, eroded,
or destroyed.

UNDER THE ARTICLES OF CONFEDERATION THE CON-
gress had been a purely federal body. Its members were

elected by the state legislatures, the states had one vote apiece, and Congress could act only through the agency of the state governments. The Constitution wrought a fundamental change by vesting the national government with power to act directly upon individuals in certain limited and specified areas, but it retained the federal principle in three of the four branches of the government it established. The Senate continued the old system, its members being elected directly by the state legislatures, and the states continued to be equally represented in it, though with two votes apiece instead of one. The president was to be elected by electors, who were to be chosen in such manner as the several state legislatures should determine; in the early elections the legislatures themselves often chose the electors and thus indirectly elected the president. Judges, being appointed by the president with the approval of the Senate, were likewise indirectly the creatures of the state legislatures, though at yet another stage of remove.

These arrangements were undone by the growth of democracy. The popular election of presidential electors was a matter of evolution: one by one the states changed their election laws until, by 1836, only the legislature of South Carolina continued to choose the electors. The popular election of senators was slower in coming: it was adopted by a number of states late in the nineteenth century and early in the twentieth, and it became a part of the Constitution upon the ratification of the Seventeenth Amendment in 1913.

The second dimension of federalism—that relating to the source of sovereignty and the nature of the union—was considerably more complex. At the time of the Revolution, there had been some disagreement as to where sovereignty devolved upon the severance of America's ties with Britain, but the matter was resolved by the way in which the Constitution was established. The Articles of Confederation had been ratified by the state legislatures, but as

Madison pointed out during the Federal Convention, a constitution ratified by the legislatures could be construed as being a treaty "among the Governments of Independent States," and thus it could be held that "a breach of any one article, by any of the parties, absolved the other parties" from any further obligation.

To avoid that construction, Madison continued, it was necessary to submit the Constitution to "the supreme authority of the people themselves." Yet it could not be submitted to the people of the United States as a whole, because the Constitution amended each of the state constitutions in various ways, and if it were adopted by majority vote of the whole people, the people in some states would be altering the constitutions of other states. This, in the nature of things, they could not have the authority to do. Accordingly, the Constitution was submitted for ratification by conventions in each of the states, delegates to which were elected by the people of the several states in their capacities as people of the several states. Madison put it thus in *Federalist* number 39: "Ratification is to be given by the people, not as individuals composing one entire nation, but as composing the distinct and independent States to which they respectively belong. It is to be the assent and ratification of the several States, derived from the supreme authority in each State,—the authority of the people themselves." This procedure unmistakably implied that the source of sovereignty was the people of the states, severally, and that the residue of sovereignty which was not committed by them to either the national government or the state governments remained in them— an implication that was subsequently made explicit by the Tenth Amendment. The process of ratification also indicated that the Union was a compact among political societies, which is to say among the people of Virginia with the people of Massachusetts with the people of Georgia, and so on.

Now, though the nature of the compact was perfectly

understood at the time, it was both subtle and unprecedented; and it is scarcely a source of wonderment that alternative formulations of what had happened were soon forthcoming. Nor is it surprising that those alternative formulations had profoundly different implications.

One of the formulations was the juristic, which was first suggested by Chief Justice John Jay but given its fullest expression by John Marshall, both as historian (in his five-volume, highly partisan biography of Washington) and as chief justice in his decision in *M'Culloch* v. *Maryland* (1819). The juristic view was that the Constitution had been created by the people as a whole, that the process of ratification by states had been resorted to only as a matter of convenience, and thus that any claims to state sovereignty or states' rights were unfounded.

The opposite view was formulated by James Madison in 1798 and was adopted by the legislature of Virginia in protest against the Alien and Sedition Acts. Conveniently forgetting what he had said earlier, Madison wrote that the federal government had resulted "from the compact to which the states are parties." From that premise it followed that when Congress enacts statutes that exceed its constitutional authority, the state governments "have the right and are in duty bound to interpose" their own authority between their citizens and the federal government, to prevent the unconstitutional enactments from being enforced. Thomas Jefferson, in the counterpart Kentucky Resolutions, referred to the federal compact as being among "sovereign and independent states."

The Virginia and Kentucky Resolutions met with a cold reception when they were proclaimed, but soon their doctrines—both about the nature of the constitutional compact and about interposition—came into widespread acceptance. It is commonly supposed that interposition was largely a southern doctrine, and the supposition is given credence by the frequency with which Virginia, Maryland, South Carolina, Kentucky, Georgia, Alabama, and other southern states defied the authority of the president, acts of Congress, treaties, and Supreme Court rulings. But it must be remembered that the legislatures of Connecticut and Massachusetts explicitly endorsed interposition in 1808; that the Hartford Convention of 1814 did likewise; that in 1840 Vermont made it a crime to aid in the capture of a runaway slave, despite the federal fugitive slave act; that in 1846 the House of Representatives of Massachusetts declared the Mexican War unconstitutional; that a decade later Wisconsin asserted the supremacy of its supreme court over the United States Supreme Court; that the official motto of Illinois was "State Sovereignty and Union." In sum, interposition was common currency throughout the country during the ante-bellum period; whether it was invoked depended, as in the adage, upon whose ox was being gored.

Meanwhile, the original, compact-among-peoples understanding was not entirely forgotten, but it was rarely appealed to because its implications were so radical. It was brought up in New England in 1805 and again in 1814, amidst talk of and as a justification for secession—a justification that no less ardent a nationalist than Gouverneur Morris declared to be sound. It arose again during the nullification controversy of 1832 / 33, with more ominous portents.

That controversy is remembered as a conflict between South Carolina and the national government and between John C. Calhoun and Andrew Jackson; the procedures that were followed, though of crucial importance, are often forgotten. Late in 1832 Governor James Hamilton called the state legislature into special session, and the legislature passed a law calling for a popularly elected state convention. The maneuver was carefully chosen. As the Constitution had been ratified in South Carolina by a popularly elected convention, the state was now returning to such a convention as the ultimate source of sovereignty. The convention met and adopted ordinances declaring the tariff acts of 1828 and 1832 null and void, forbidding appeal to the Supreme Court in cases arising under the ordinances, and asserting that the state would have just cause for seceding from the Union if the national government should attempt to use force to collect the tariff.

The outcome of the confrontation was indecisive. Congress backed down, passing Henry Clay's compromise tariff; but it also enacted Jackson's Force Bill, which authorized the president to use the army against South Carolina if it continued to defy the law. The state, for its part, rescinded its nullification ordinances, but it also formally nullified the Force Bill.

South Carolina's position was what in the eighteenth century was called a "return to first principles," and when it was adopted, it could be refuted only by the sword. And it was adopted during the winter of 1860/61: each of the eleven seceding states left the Union the way the original thirteen states had entered into it, by means of conventions elected by the people for the purpose. The defeat of the Confederacy in the Civil War resolved the issue for all time, though not immediately. Radicals in Congress first insisted that the southern states had committed political suicide by seceding and that they were therefore to be treated as "conquered provinces." Subsequently, however, the Radicals realized that the votes of the southern states would probably be necessary to ensure the ratification of the Fourteenth Amendment. Accordingly, they reversed themselves and—on condition that the amendment be ratified—now held that the states had never left the Union. The Supreme Court confirmed that interpretation in the case of *Texas* v. *White* (1869). Disregarding the fact that Virginia had been dismembered, in palpable violation of the Constitution, by the creation of West Virginia in 1863, the Court ruled that the Constitution "looks to an indestructible Union, composed of indestructible states."

Unintentionally, however, in rendering that decision the Court reconfirmed the Madisonian-Jeffersonian interpretation of the Constitution as a compact among state governments and thereby left the door open for a revival of the doctrine of interposition. Despite the Fourteenth Amendment, the southern states were able, late in the nineteenth century and early in the twentieth, to deprive their black citizens of most of their civil rights; and when the Court began trying to restore those rights during the 1950s and 1960s, interposition barred the way. None of the southern states officially embraced the doctrine, though a number of people urged them to do so; but as a practical matter the southern governors and legislatures resisted desegregation by doing precisely what Madison had called for in 1798. Their efforts succeeded only in discrediting what, in other and more morally defensible contexts, was a valid and valuable protection against the encroachments of the national government—even as South Carolina's position had been discredited in defense of slavery a century earlier.

THE THIRD DIMENSION OF FEDERALISM AROSE FROM the fact that the Framers of the Constitution did something that political theorists since ancient times had insisted could not be done, which is to say, divide sovereignty. In the eighteenth century, sovereignty was defined as the supreme law-making power; as Blackstone said, "Sovereignty and legislature are indeed convertible terms." Having two sovereignties in the same territory was obviously impossible. The Framers worked their way around that stumbling block by attacking the problem in an ingenious way. Conceiving of sovereignty, not as a single power, but as an aggregate of many specific powers, they could allocate those specific powers among different governments and among different branches of the same government. Each government or branch of government had, in Hamilton's words, "sovereign power as to *certain things*, and not as to *other things.*"

The Constitution bestowed sovereign powers upon the national government only in regard to a handful of general objects. All other powers, except those that were forbidden to both national and state governments, remained in the hands of the states. As Madison explained in *Federalist* number 45: "The powers delegated by the . . . Constitution to the federal government are few and defined. Those which are to remain in the State governments are numerous and indefinite. The former will be exercised principally on external objects, as war, peace, negotiation, and foreign commerce; with which last the power of taxation will, for the most part, be connected. The powers reserved to the several States will extend to all the objects which, in the ordinary course of affairs, concern the lives, liberties, and properties of the people, and the internal order, improvement, and prosperity of the State." These state powers were commonly referred to as the power of "internal police," or simply the police power, which included the definition and punishment of crimes, the administration of justice, the governance of property rights and relationships, and the regulation of all matters concerning the health, manners, morals, safety, and welfare of the citizenry. The national government had no police power, and such powers as it did have were further curtailed by the adoption of the Bill of Rights—which imposed limitations on the national government but not on the state governments.

Despite Article VI, which declares the Constitution and congressional enactments passed in pursuance thereof to be the supreme law of the land, the preponderance of powers thus lay with the states, and most states insisted from the outset that all disputes about which governments could do what should be decided in favor of the states. As early as 1790, Virginia was challenging what it saw as congressional usurpation of powers reserved to the states, provoking Alexander Hamilton to declare that this was "the first symptom of a spirit which must either be killed or will kill the constitution." The very first decision in which the Supreme Court ruled against a state—that in *Chisholm* v. *Georgia* (1793)—resulted in a constitutional amendment curtailing the Court's jurisdiction and protecting the sovereignty of the states against suits by foreigners or citizens of other states. Repeatedly during Marshall's tenure (1801–35) the Court ruled that the states could not constitutionally do one thing or another, and the states did them anyway. Under Chief Justice Roger Brooke Taney (1836–64) the Court erected a virtual wall of separation around the states. The adoption of the Fourteenth Amendment in 1868 provided features that might have been employed to curtail state power, but apart from the relatively minor restrictions imposed under the doctrine of substantive due process, the states continued to be the principal units of government until well into the twentieth century. A rough indication of the relative importance of the levels of government can be expressed statistically: as late as 1929, state and local governments had nearly five times as many employees as the national government had (nearly ten times as many if post-office personnel are excluded) and spent three times as much money.

The process by which the balance of federal and state powers was overturned was long and involved, but the major phases can be described under three broad headings. First came the evolution of a national police power. The police power had resided exclusively in the states, and it had been consistently upheld by the Court even when there were conflicts with other constitutional provisions, as there were, for example, in *Stone* v. *Mississippi* (1880) and *Holden* v. *Hardy* (1898). But just after the turn of the century, Congress passed an act prohibiting the interstate transportation of lottery tickets and an act imposing a tax on oleomargarine, the latter on the pretext that margarine was dangerous to the health. In upholding these acts in 1903 and 1904, the Supreme Court ruled for the first time that the national government does in fact have a police power. The passage of the Pure Food and Drug Act and the Meat Inspection Act soon followed. Other such legislation steadily accumulated, and between 1937 and 1957—during which period the Court declared only one act of Congress unconstitutional—the whole range of police-power legislation was invaded by Congress.

A second group of developments was fiscal. The adoption of the Sixteenth Amendment, authorizing taxes on incomes; the passage of the Glass-Steagall Act of 1932, basing federal-reserve note currency upon governmental debt; and the abandonment of the gold standard; all these combined to make possible virtually unlimited and uncontrollable spending by the national government. Closely related to that development and in part growing out of it was the emergence of revenue sharing in one form and another—the subsidization of state and local governments by the national government and the ever-increasing dependence of the first two upon the last. It is to be observed that southerners, despite their traditional adherence to federalism and states' rights, did not resist this turn of events and were indeed in the vanguard of bringing it about. As the Bible puts it, they proved willing to sell their birthright for a mess of pottage. (A very large mess, but a mess nonetheless.)

The final blows were wielded by the Supreme Court, largely through the doctrine of incorporation, which runs roughly as follows. The Bill of Rights, as originally passed and as interpreted by the courts for 134 years, restricted the federal government but did not apply to the state governments. Then in 1925 the Court declared, in its decision in the case of *Gitlow v. New York*, that the Fourteenth Amendment's protection of liberty against state interference extended some of the fundamental liberties guaranteed by the Bill of Rights to apply to the states. For a time, the consequences of that declaration were minimal; the Court was loath to determine just what was a "fundamental" liberty. The conviction of Gitlow for publishing Communist propaganda in violation of a New York law, for instance, was upheld on the ground that freedom of speech is not an absolute right. A number of other cases were settled in similar fashion during the next dozen years; they culminated in a case in which the Court ruled that the Fifth Amendment's protection against double jeopardy was not a fundamental liberty. The Court continued to be cautious about applying the doctrine of incorporation throughout the 1940s and the 1950s. Indeed, it was not until 1961 that incorporation began to be applied on a grand scale, but since that time the Court has manufactured "fundamental rights" with reckless abandon. The result has been that control over matters of local concern has been transferred from local and state governments to the national government in Washington.

Constitutional traditionalists, especially in the South, have been incensed by most of this, and much of the relevant litigation has arisen in the South. The rights of accused criminals were established in suits originating in Arizona and Illinois; but both pioneering abortion cases, many of the landmark cases concerning school prayer, some of the most important affirmative-active cases, and all of the major legislative-reapportionment cases were southern in origin.

There are some ironies in all this. Among the foremost apostles of the doctrine of incorporation, especially in regard to First Amendment rights, was the next-to-the-last southerner to sit on the Supreme Court, Hugo Black of Alabama. But Black, toward the end of his long and distinguished career, at last came to recognize the dangers inherent in carrying the principle too far. In a dissenting opinion in 1968 he pointed out that the nation had always understood "that it could be more tranquil and orderly if it functioned on the principle that the local communities should control their own peculiar affairs under their own particular rules." In 1970, the year before he died, he warned that if the Court did not exercise restraint, it would destroy the federal system created by the Constitution by reducing the state governments to "impotent figureheads."

The larger irony is this. Political scientists and historians are in agreement that federalism is the greatest contribution of the Founding Fathers to the science of government. It is also the only feature of the Constitution that has been successfully exported, that can be employed to protect liberty elsewhere in the world. Yet what we invented, and others imitate, no longer exists on its native shores.

INDEX